YOUNG GUNS

YOUNG GUNS

TRIUMPH
BOOKS
CHICAGO

Authors:

Woody Cain is a journalist living in Concord, North Carolina with his wife, Sandy. A graduate of Appalachian State University, he has covered motorsports for radio, television, and print since 1987. Cain is host of the live call-in television program *Let's Talk Racing*, and play-by-play announcer for the televised *Around the Track* racing productions and specials.

Other professional credits include work as a general reporter and editor for daily, weekly, and monthly publications, as well as radio news/sports director at WEGO-AM in Concord and WABZ-FM in Albemarle, North Carolina. Cain currently works as editor of *The Charlotte Observer's University City Magazine* in Charlotte, North Carolina.

Jason Mitchell is a veteran NASCAR Winston Cup Series freelance writer who resides in Concord, North Carolina.

Mitchell was born August 14, 1972, in Fort Walton Beach, Florida. While he was young, Mitchell's family moved to North Wilkesboro, North Carolina. His love for auto racing began while growing up around the now-defunct North Wilkesboro Speedway, which until 1996 hosted two NASCAR Winston Cup Series races a year.

Mitchell graduated from Appalachian State University in Boone, North Carolina, in 1996 with a bachelor of science degree in communications. He majored in public relations with a minor in marketing.

Upon graduation, Mitchell became assistant sports editor at the *Wilkes Journal-Patriot*. Trying to get closer to the "hub" of racing in and around Charlotte, North Carolina, Mitchell moved and spent four years as the motorsports writer with the *Independent Tribune* in Concord.

Mitchell's freelance writing has been included in *Stock Car Racing* magazine, *NASCAR Magazine*, *Inside NASCAR*, *Racing Milestones*, *Last Lap*, as well as program work for Lowe's Motor Speedway and International Speedway Corporation. Some of Mitchell's technical writing has appeared on NASCAR.com.

David Poole has covered NASCAR for *The Charlotte Observer* since 1997. He has won awards for his coverage from the Associated Press Sports Editors and the National Motorsports Press Association. He was the winner of the George Cunningham Award as the NMPA's writer of the year in 2001. Poole is a graduate of the University of North Carolina and lives in his hometown of Gastonia, North Carolina, with his wife, Karen, and her three children, Matthew, David, and Emily.

Photography:
The Charlotte Observer
Brain L. Spurlock, Spurlock Photography Inc.
Joe Robbins

Editor:
Constance Holloway

Design Team:
Larry Preslar
Beth Epperly
Andrea Ross

This book is available in quantity at special discounts for your group or organization. For further information, contact:
Triumph Books
601 South LaSalle Street
Suite 500
Chicago, Illinois 60605
(312) 939-3330
Fax (312) 663-3557

Printed in the United States of America
ISBN 1-57243-522-4

Driver Biography   7

Jeff Gordon

Jeff Gordon is the driver of the No. 24 Dupont Chevy in the NASCAR Winston Cup Series.

Born: August 4, 1971
Hometown Born: Vallejo, California
Resides: Mooresville, North Carolina
Spouse: Brooke

DID YOU KNOW? Gordon set the all-time record for consecutive victories on road courses (six) with his win at Sears Point in June 2000.

CAREER HIGHLIGHTS:
2002 Outlook: With his team intact, Gordon's future appears as bright as ever.

2001: Gordon posted victories in the Kmart 400, UAW-DaimlerChrysler 400 at Las Vegas, MBNA Platinum 400 at Dover, Brickyard 400 at Indianapolis, Global Crossing @ The Glen, and the Protection One 400 at Kansas Speedway. He won his 4th series championship behind six wins and six poles. He also won The Winston all-star race and surpassed the late Dale Earnhardt in career earnings.

2000 and 1999: Lackluster seasons—by Gordon's standards—saw him slip to 6th and 9th in the standings.

Dale Earhardt Jr.

Dale Earnhardt Jr. is the driver of the No. 8 Budweiser Chevy in the NASCAR Winston Cup Series.

Born: October 10, 1974
Hometown Born: Kannapolis, North Carolina
Resides: Mooresville, North Carolina
Martial Status: Single

DID YOU KNOW? Earnhardt won the NASCAR Grand National series championship in 1998 and 1999.

CAREER HIGHLIGHTS
2002 Outlook: The added experience and strong second-half performance last season leave Earnhardt Jr. in a good position to battle for the championship.

2001: Three wins—the Pepsi 400, MBNA Cal Ripken Jr. 400, and EA Sports 500—provided Earnhardt Jr. and his team a strong burst of momentum.

2000: In his first full season, he won two poles and two races, but lost the Rookie-of-the-Year battle to Matt Kenseth. He also won The Winston all-star race.

1999: He ran five Winston Cup events, with a best start of 8th and a best finish of 10th.

Tony Stewart

Date of Birth: May 20, 1971
Hometown Born: Rushville, Indiana
Resides: Lake Norman, North Carolina, and Columbus, Indiana
Marital Status: Single
Height: 5'9"
Weight: 165 pounds
Hobbies: Racing, boating, bowling, and shooting pool

CAREER HIGHLIGHTS
1995: Became only driver in history to win United States Auto (USAC) Club's version of the "Triple Crown" by winning championships in the National Midget, Sprint, and Silver Crown divisions.

1996: Won the pole for the Indianapolis 500

1997: Indy Racing League season championship

1998: Competed in 22 NASCAR Busch Grand National races, winning two poles along with accumulating five top-five and five top-ten finishes. Also competed in the IRL division, finishing third in the final standings thanks to two victories and four poles.

1999: Became the first driver in NASCAR Winston Cup Series history to win three races during his rookie season while driving for Joe Gibbs Racing in the No. 20 Home Depot Pontiac. First career victory came at Richmond on September 11, 1999. Finished fourth in the final point standings while earning Winston Cup Rookie of the Year honors. Stewart's other two victories came at Phoenix and Homestead-Miami.

2000: Stewart won a career-best six races during his sophomore effort. Won two more poles and finished sixth in the final points. Stewart's victories included a sweep of both races at Dover, as well as wins at Michigan, Homestead, New Hampshire, and Martinsville.

2001: Continuing to improve, Stewart finished a career-best second in the final standings. Started the season by beating Dale Earnhardt to win the Budweiser Shootout, only days before the fatal last-lap crash in the Daytona 500 that claimed the life of the seven-time Winston Cup champion. Also won for the second time at Richmond before winning the night race at Bristol. His career earnings in only three full Winston Cup seasons surpassed the $11 million mark.

*2002: Stewart won at Atlanta in only the fourth race of the season. Continued his love affair with Richmond by winning at the short track in the spring, marking his 14th career Winston Cup victory. Picked up his fifth career pole position in June at Infineon Raceway in Sears Point. *2002 statistics through June 23*

Matt Kenseth

Matt Kenseth is the driver of the No. 17 DeWalt Tools Ford in the NASCAR Winston Cup Series for Roush Racing.

Born: January 10, 1972
Hometown Born: Cambridge, Wisconsin
Resides: Terrell, North Carolina
Spouse: Katie
Children: Ross
Height: 5'9"
Weight: 152 pounds
Hobbies: Computer games, motorcycling, golf, and boating

DID YOU KNOW? Despite the fact that Kenseth hasn't yet raced three full seasons at the Winston Cup level, he has earned more than $7 million in winnings.

CAREER HIGHLIGHTS
2002: At the midway point of the season, Kenseth had three victories to lead the Winston Cup circuit while sitting 10th in the standings and well within striking distance of the front five drivers. Kenseth picked up the second Winston Cup victory of his career in the second race of the season at Rockingham. Backed that up with victories at Texas and Michigan. Kenseth won his first career pole position at Dover.

2001: Somewhat of a disappointing year for Kenseth, who went without a win before finishing 13th in the final Winston Cup point standings. Only four top-five finishes during the season and failed to finish five races. Qualifying was a contributing factor as the team had only six efforts of 20th or better in 36 races. Kenseth helped his team win the season's Pit Crew Competition championship held each autumn in Rockingham.

2000: Kenseth earned the Winston Cup Rookie-of-the-Year award in one of the toughest battles for that honor in NASCAR history over rival and close friend Dale Earnhardt Jr. Scored his first career victory in the Coca-Cola 600 at Lowe's Motor Speedway, winning NASCAR's longest race in his first start. The Kenseth camp finished the season 14th in the final point standings.

1999: Kenseth drove in five races for Roush Racing in preparation for his rookie season. Scored a best finish of fourth at Dover.

1998: Kenseth drove in relief at Dover for veteran Bill Elliott so he could attend his father's funeral. In only his first Winston Cup start, Kenseth ended up with a solid sixth-place finish.

Jimmie Johnson

Jimmie Johnson is the driver of the No. 48 Lowe's Chevrolet in the NASCAR Winston Cup Series for Hendrick Motorsports.

Born: September 17, 1975
Hometown Born: El Cajon, California
Resides: Mooresville, North Carolina
Marital Status: Single
Height: 5'11"
Weight: 175 pounds
Hobbies: Water sports

DID YOU KNOW? During the 2000 season, Johnson was selected as one of People magazine's "Sexiest Men in the Fast Lane," along with other Winston Cup and Busch Series drivers.

CAREER HIGHLIGHTS
2002: At the season's halfway point, Johnson sat an impressive third in the Winston Cup point standings and a mere 89 points behind leader Sterling Marlin. Picked up his first career Winston Cup victory in April at California Speedway, backing that up a month later by winning at Dover. Johnson has won three poles through the first 18 races, including the top spot for the season-opening Daytona 500. Also was the fastest qualifier at Talladega and Charlotte. Leads Ryan Newman by a 265-237 margin in the battle for the Rookie-of-the-Year award, posting better finishes in eleven races compared to seven for Newman.

2001: Made his Winston Cup debut at Lowe's Motor Speedway after a 15th-place qualifying run at Lowe's Motor Speedway in a car owned by Rick Hendrick. Started three Winston Cup events with a best finish of 25th at Homestead. Also ran entire Busch Series schedule and finished eighth in the final point standings driving for Herzog Motorsports. Earned his first Busch Series victory at Chicago.

2000: Johnson ran his first full season in the Busch Series, finishing an impressive 10th in the final standings and third in the Rookie-of-the-Year battle. Best finish of the year was sixth at Homestead.

Kevin Harvick

Kevin Harvick is the driver of the No. 29 Goodwrench Chevrolet in the NASCAR Winston Cup Series.

Born: December 8, 1975
Hometown Born: Bakersfield, California
Resides: Winston-Salem, North Carolina
Spouse: DeLana
Height: 5'10"
Weight: 175 pounds
Hobbies: Radio-controlled race cars

DID YOU KNOW? Kevin and his wife, DeLana, were married in Las Vegas in February 2001, two days after he made his Winston Cup debut at Rockingham.

CAREER HIGHLIGHTS
2002: Won the third NASCAR Winston Cup Series race of his career at Chicagoland Speedway, his second victory in two starts at the Chicago track.

2001: Under trying emotional circumstances following the death of seven-time Winston Cup champion Dale Earnhardt, Harvick took over the vacated ride and edged Jeff Gordon in a photo finish at Atlanta in only his third career start. In addition to running each Winston Cup race following the Daytona 500, Harvick was also trying to win the Busch Series championship. Performing remarkably considering both schedules, Harvick would go on to win the inaugural Winston Cup race at Chicago before clinching the Busch Series championship. Finished ninth in Winston Cup points despite missing Daytona. By the time the year was over, Harvick had logged more than 20,000 miles at 30 different tracks. As a result, he earned over $6 million in total winnings on the season. Harvick won the season-opening IROC (International Race of Champions) event at Daytona International Speedway.

Kurt Busch

Kurt Busch is the driver of the No. 97 Rubbermaid Ford in the NASCAR Winston Cup Series for Roush Racing.

Born: August 4, 1974
Hometown Born: Las Vegas, Nevada
Resides: Concord, North Carolina
Marital Status: Single
Height: 5'11"
Weight: 150 pounds
Hobbies: Jet skiing, water-skiing, snow skiing

DID YOU KNOW? Busch prefers alternative music and says his favorite band is Metallica. His favorite actor is Tom Cruise, and Sandra Bullock is his favorite actress.

CAREER HIGHLIGHTS
2002: In only his second full season of racing in the NASCAR Winston Cup Series, Busch picked up his first career victory in the Food City 500 at Bristol Motor Speedway. At the season's halfway point Busch sat ninth in the Winston Cup point standings, second best of all the Roush Racing drivers. Mark Martin was 2nd in the standings, with Matt Kenseth just one position behind Busch in 10th, while Burton was 18th.

2001: In his rookie season on the Winston Cup Series tour, Busch turned in a respectable effort while learning the ropes at NASCAR's top level. Ended up 27th in the final Winston Cup standings while finishing in the top-five three times and the top-ten a total of six times. His best finish was a third-place effort in the spring race at Talladega. Also posted an impressive fifth-place finish in the Brickyard 400 at Indianapolis. Busch picked up his first career Winston Cup pole for the Southern 500 at Darlington.

2000: Entered seven NASCAR Winston Cup Series races in order to maintain his rookie status in a Ford owned by Roush Racing, while also driving full time for Roush in the Craftsman Truck Series and going to victory lane four times.

Ryan Newman

Ryan Newman is the driver of the No. 12 Alltel Ford in the NASCAR Winston Cup Series.

Name: Ryan Newman
Born: December 8, 1977
Hometown Born: South Bend, Indiana
Resides: Sherrills Ford, North Carolina
Marital Status: Single
Height: 5'11"
Weight: 207 pounds
Hobbies: Radio-controlled cars and fishing

DID YOU KNOW? Newman is a 2001 graduate of Purdue University with a bachelor of science degree in vehicle-structure engineering. At Purdue, Newman was the recipient of the Rich Vogler Memorial Scholarship. He is also a member of the Quarter Midget Hall of Fame thanks to his success as a young up-and-coming driver in the USAC ranks.

CAREER HIGHLIGHTS
2002: At the midway point of Newman's first full season, he was in second place in the Rookie-of-the-Year standings. He had 237 points and was 28 points away from first place. Jimmie Johnson's strong point has been two victories, while Newman has yet to win a Winston Cup race. Newman, however, did win The Winston all-star race in May at Lowe's Motor Speedway. Also won poles at California and Chicago.

2001: Ran a limited Winston Cup schedule in order to maintain Rookie-of-the-Year status. In only his third Winston Cup career start, Newman grabbed his first pole in the Coca-Cola 600 at Lowe's Motor Speedway. His best finish in eight races came with a second-place effort at Chicagoland Speedway. Also ran 15 Busch Series races, winning at Michigan International Speedway in only his ninth start. Newman picked up six poles. Won the season-opening ARCA race at Daytona International Speedway.

The Kid with the Moustache

Before Jeff Gordon burst onto the scene in 1993, accepted wisdom said stock car drivers were born and raised under the shade trees of the South, where they worked on cars then took them to their local short track on Saturday nights.

The better ones progressed through the ranks over the years with a lot of grease and hard luck along the way. The best of those, if they were fortunate enough to convince someone—anyone—to give them a shot at the big time, went racing for NASCAR's Winston Cup.

Gordon seemed to tilt the status quo on its ear. Since he had come up through the Midget and Sprint Car ranks, many longtime NASCAR

fans had never heard of him. Some even scoffed at his chances for success when he made the move to stock cars in 1991.

Despite Gordon's array of accomplishments, NASCAR insiders privately expressed amusement in fall 1990 when he visited Charlotte (now Lowe's) Motor Speedway for an open practice session to test a Grand National car.

"That absolutely is the youngest kid I've ever seen with a moustache," said one.

Born August 4, 1971, in Vallejo, California, and raised in Pittsboro, Indiana, Gordon began his racing career at five years old when his stepfather, John Bickford, put him in a Quarter Midget car after his mother worried

BMX bicycle racing might be too dangerous. He flipped the car five times practicing for his first organized race but came back to set the fastest qualifying time.

Winning soon became a way of life. Later, his family moved to Indiana when California age restrictions started limiting where he could race. By age 19 he was the youngest champion ever in the U.S. Auto Club's Midget series.

By the time he was 20 he had twice been named to the All-American Team by the American Racing Writers and Broadcasters Association, joining such legends as Dale Earnhardt, Harry Gant, Michael Andretti, and Rick Mears.

Gordon paid his dues by winning four national go-kart class championships, Quarter-Midget national championships in 1979 and 1981, a U.S. Auto Club Midget championship in 1990, and the 1991 USAC Silver Crown championship trophy. He won more than 500 short track events, many of them televised on ESPN's Saturday Night Thunder series, bringing him national popularity.

When he was granted his USAC racing license on his 16th birthday, Gordon became the youngest-ever driver on that circuit, and he posted 22 wins, 21 poles, 55 top-five finishes, and 66 top-10 finishes over 93 starts in four divisions.

Opting for a NASCAR career over open-wheel Indy Car racing, Gordon came south in 1991 to drive Fords for team owner Bill Davis on the Grand National tour. He didn't win that first season, but his diamond-in-the-rough talent was apparent. He finished second three times and third once. He had five top-five and 10 top-10 finishes, won one pole position and two outside poles, and wound up 11th overall in the point standings, earning Rookie-of-the-Year honors.

In a 300-miler at Atlanta Motor Speedway in March 1992, Gordon drove to his first NASCAR checkered flag.

"The last lap, I almost lost the race because I was so choked up all the way around," said Gordon.

He had no way of knowing it at the time, but his showing that day was to lead to a dramatic turn in his career. Gordon added two more victories that season, taking both 300-milers at Charlotte Motor Speedway from the pole. Overall, he won 11 poles, a Grand National single-season record.

In the first Charlotte win in May, Gordon pulled a daring pass for the lead that would have made any stock car racing veteran proud and charged to a victory in the Champion 300. The triumph was worth a NASCAR Grand National Series record purse of $115,125 for Gordon, 20, and the Bill Davis team. It undoubtedly meant an even bigger marketing bonanza for Ford, which was winless in 33 Grand National races at Charlotte until Gordon flashed under the checkered flag that day.

A sheet-metal-scrubbing pass of veteran Dick Trickle in Turn 4 on the 163rd of the race's 200 laps was the key; Gordon steadily pulled away from there. It was a risky three-cars-wide maneuver, as Phil Parsons' lapped Oldsmobile was also involved.

"I had a lot of close calls out there," said Gordon. "That pass was one of them. We were rubbing, but rubbing is racing."

There seemed no doubt Gordon would graduate to the Winston Cup Series in 1993 with Davis and Ford, who had championed his entry to NASCAR. However, at a race in Nazareth, Pennsylvania, word leaked that Gordon had signed to join Hendrick Motorsports, a Chevrolet operation, in 1993. Through an incredible oversight, Ford officials hadn't protected the company in the phenom's contract.

Controversy ensued. Ford threatened to sue but never did, and Gordon moved to

12

Charlotte to join team owner Rick Hendrick. The determination of Hendrick to hire Jeff Gordon as a driver was inspired that cold spring Saturday when the youngster was en route to victory in the Atlanta 300-miler.

"I was on my way to a VIP suite in Turn 1 and the cars were going by right under us," recalled Hendrick. "This one guy had his car so sideways in the corner that smoke was boiling from the rear tires every lap.

"I told a friend that was with me, 'Just watch. In a lap or two that guy's going to bust "I said to myself right then that I wanted a fellow with the ability to handle a car like that driving for me."

Up To Cup

Jeff Gordon made his NASCAR Winston Cup Series debut in the 1992 season finale, the final race of Richard Petty's driving career.

Gordon broke into Winston Cup in 1993 more sensationally than even Hendrick could have imagined. He won a 125-mile qualifying race at Daytona International Speedway, experiencing a fateful introduction to victory lane. He then dogged Dale Earnhardt's bumper for much of the Daytona 500 before Dale Jarrett passed them both on the last lap. Gordon wound up fifth in the 500, an auspicious debut.

To his disappointment, Gordon didn't win a regular-season race in his first year, but he was runner-up twice, had five other top-five finishes, and four other top 10s en route to $765, 168 in winnings, 14th place in the points standings, and the Rookie-of-the-Year title.

There was no doubt 1994 would be a sensational season for Gordon, young enough to be the son of many of his rivals. It exceeded expectations.

First came victory in February's Busch Clash, a race at Daytona matching the previous season's pole winners. Finally, amidst deep drama, came a regular-season win.

Through the Coca-Cola 600 at Charlotte in May, Rusty Wallace and Geoff Bodine dueled for the lead, with Gordon lurking a bit behind in his No. 24 Chevy with the brilliant, multicolored paint scheme.

With a record crowd watching the first nighttime finish of the classic, Bodine and Wallace pitted for four tires and fuel. Then Gordon came onto pit road and was out in a flash. Crew chief Ray Evernham had called for only right-side tires, a brilliant decision that put Gordon in the lead. He never gave it up.

"That pit stop won the race for us," said Gordon afterward. "It was a great call.

"Ray and I talk a lot about the things we want to do in racing, and one of them was that we didn't want to sneak up on our first win—

get it because someone wrecked or got a yellow flag at the wrong time. We wanted to go out there and beat them on the race track or in the pits. We wanted to do it the way it is supposed to be done."

As huge as the Charlotte triumph was for Gordon and his team, a larger one awaited on August 6.

For more than eight decades, the only auto race held at Indianapolis Motor Speedway was the Indianapolis 500. Eventually, NASCAR's explosion in popularity made it inevitable that

a Winston Cup event would be held at the 2.5-mile track. The Brickyard 400 was born.

"Everyone was excited to be racing at Indy, me especially since I'd grown up nearby," said Gordon. "I was really hopeful of running well.

"The first lap in practice I knew we had a great car. I felt we had a shot at the pole, but I slipped and we wound up third, and I was pretty happy with that. In practice the next day, there wasn't anybody I couldn't run down."

During the race, attended by a NASCAR-record crowd estimated at 300,000, Gordon

battled with Geoff Bodine for the lead until Bodine was sidelined by a bumping incident with his brother, Brett. Then Ernie Irvan, moving up from the middle of the pack, engaged Gordon in a thrilling duel until Irvan cut a tire with five laps to go. Gordon then held Brett Bodine at bay to become the first Brickyard 400 winner, assuring a prominent place in motorsports history.

"That inaugural race was bigger than life as far as I'm concerned," said Gordon, who won a NASCAR-record $613,000. "I didn't know how much the race paid until the next day when I saw the paper.

"The money means nothing to me. . . . I'm sure I'll enjoy it, but the main thing to any guy in the facility driving a race car that day is that he wanted to win the race, no matter what.

"There's only going to be one guy to win the first one, take that checkered flag, and drive into victory lane to enjoy that excitement. We were that team and I was that guy. There wasn't anybody in the world that I'd have traded places with at that moment.

"I guess if you look at the race in a certain way, it looked like it was fixed, me being from Indiana and all. But it really wasn't. NASCAR didn't give us any more breaks than anybody else."

A Champion Emerges

By April 1995, Gordon was being taken seriously as a threat for the Winston Cup championship. He won the pole for the First Union 400 at North Wilkesboro Speedway, his fourth pole in the first seven races.

An all-Ford front row of Brett Bodine and Derrike Cope seemed likely at the five-eighths-mile track until Gordon took his Monte Carlo on the track 43rd among 45 qualifiers. He edged Bodine as rivals shook their heads.

In four previous races at North Wilkesboro, Gordon had qualified 7th, 16th, 12th, and 12th. Bodine's bid in a Thunderbird fielded by local hero Junior Johnson brought a roar from several thousand fans hoping to see his team break out of a slump.

The North Wilkesboro pole seemed to set afire discussion of a possible championship run. There was an obvious growing rivalry with Dale Earnhardt, the seven-time champion who for years had been Chevy's ace.

Gordon didn't win that North Wilkesboro race; he finished second to Earnhardt.

In May, Gordon added to his growing legend by winning The Winston Select all-star race, leading all three segments of the wreck-marred event at Charlotte.

Two months later he won a final-lap sprint in the Pepsi 400 at Daytona International Speedway. The win was the fourth of the Winston Cup season for Gordon, but his first in a series championship event at Daytona's 2.5-mile track.

By August, when the series headed back to Indy, Gordon was all the rage. He wanted to finish the season with a win at Atlanta to wrap up the title, but defending-series champion Dale Earnhardt scored a dominating victory in the NAPA 500. It wasn't enough to overtake Gordon for the NASCAR Winston Cup championship, however, worth at least $1.3 million. Gordon clinched a first title for himself and Hendrick Motorsports.

FIERCE COMPETITOR

In 1996 Gordon entered the NASCAR Winston Cup Series racing season with the goal of winning the circuit's championship.

Gordon won 10 races and had a 110-point lead over teammate Terry Labonte with four races left. Labonte won his second championship by winning at Charlotte and finishing third at Rockingham and Phoenix, then driving to a fifth-place finish in the season finale at Atlanta. Labonte edged Gordon by 37 points for the title.

The next year brought one of the closest championship finishes in the history of the Winston Cup Series. Gordon won the season-opening Daytona 500, then made it two in a row with a win the following week at Rockingham.

At Bristol in April 1997, Gordon muscled his Chevrolet past short-track ace Rusty Wallace's Ford in the final turn to win the Food City 500. Gordon chased Wallace down during a heart-stopping, 50-lap green flag fight to the finish that followed a 450-lap demolition derby.

After fending off Labonte's effort to pass him for second, Gordon closed on Wallace's rear bumper down the backstretch on the final lap and the cars made contact in the final set of turns.

Gordon's short-track style tap pushed Wallace just high enough for Gordon to dive inside and get to the finish line first by less than a half second.

Gordon made it two straight wins again at Martinsville the next week, surviving a 360-degree spin to score a dominating victory in the Goody's 500.

In September 1997, one lap away from $1 million, Jeff Gordon looked in his mirror and saw Jeff Burton coming. In the week before the Southern 500 at Darlington Raceway, Gordon told everybody what would happen if he found himself in that situation.

What it took was a fender-banging battle down the front stretch under the white flag and into the first turn of the final lap, with Gordon edging Burton to become the second driver to win the "Winston Million" bonus.

Gordon needed to win the Southern 500 to go with his wins at Daytona and Charlotte that season to claim the Winston Million, a bonus for winning any three of the so-called "Big Four" races on the NASCAR Winston Cup circuit.

He won it the hard way: by enduring four hours of racing that turned into an epic of banging and slamming and narrow escapes.

The most significant thing about the victory wasn't the million bucks. It was that Gordon, at age 26, won the Southern 500, the most demanding test in stock car racing, for the third year in a row.

STRETCH RUN

Entering the last five races of 1997, Gordon led Martin by 135 points and Dale Jarrett by 222. Jarrett won at Charlotte and Martin was fourth, but Gordon finished fifth. At Talladega the next week a 23-car pile-up ensued when

Gordon blew a tire and slashed across the track, starting a chain reaction that damaged every car in the top five in points. Terry Labonte won and Gordon finished 35th. Jarrett wound up 21st and Martin come home 30th. Both missed a chance to make up ground in the points battle.

From there it was on to Rockingham, where Bobby Hamilton won in a race held on Monday after rain postponed the event a day earlier. Jarrett finished second and Martin sixth, but Gordon held his pursuers at bay with a fourth-place finish. Jarrett won his seventh race of the year the next week at Phoenix and Martin drove to sixth, but Gordon battled back to 17th after a late flat tire forced him to pit under green. Jarrett and Martin were within 100 points with one race left: Atlanta.

Gordon started off by spinning into Hamilton on pit road during practice, forcing the 24 team to a backup car. Bobby Labonte won the race while Jarrett and Martin came in second and third. Gordon fought his way to

17th again—enough to win the championship by just 14 over Jarrett and 29 over Martin—the closest battle among three drivers for the title in series history. It also represented the third straight title for Hendrick Motorsports. The $1.5 million championship check and other season-ending awards pushed Gordon's 1997 winnings close to $6 million, erasing the single-season record of $4.3 million he set in

By now, Gordon had appeared in a commercial with Shaquille O'Neal. He'd done the TV talk thing with David Letterman and Jay Leno. He was interviewed by Cindy Crawford and was on *People* magazine's list of the "50 most beautiful people." He signed a deal with the William Morris Agency, joining Crawford, Bruce Willis, Bill Cosby, and John Travolta on that agency's list of clients.

NASCAR's 50th-anniversary season kicked off in 1998 with Dale Earnhardt's first-ever Daytona 500 win. Earnhardt dominated a 125-mile qualifying race before the 500 and Gordon won an International Race of Champions event leading up to NASCAR's Super Bowl. Earnhardt's winnings of $1 million smashed Gordon's record Winston Cup race winner's purse of $613,000 for winning the 1994 Brickyard 400.

The next week Gordon bounced back at Rockingham, coming from well behind to win the Goodwrench 400. The No. 24 Chevrolet Monte Carlo was so loose that Gordon fell as far back as 31st before fighting back to win his 30th race.

At Bristol in March a rapid-fire pit stop by his Rainbow Warriors crew helped Gordon gain critical track position and sent him on his way to victory in the Food City 500—his fourth straight victory in the track's spring race. Gordon survived two late cautions and other scrapes as he led the final 63 laps to become the first two-time winner of the season.

At Charlotte in May, The Winston all-star race provided a bizarre twist in its 14th running. Mark Martin scored his first career victory in the event in a Ford that was unquestionably strong, but outclassed, before Gordon's Chevrolet sputtered and died as it went into Turn 1 on the final lap.

"I'm afraid to say it, but we ran out of gas, I think," Gordon said.

Martin passed Bobby Labonte to take second place as they came out of the fourth turn and headed for the white flag. Gordon was ahead by more than a second, though, and appeared to be heading for a second straight win and his third in four years in the event. When Gordon's car slowed, Martin sailed by for the win.

As the cars came to start the final 10-lap segment, Gordon was leading, but he got started too quickly. The start was waved off and the cars circled the track under yellow. Had it not been for that extra distance, Gordon's car might have run out of gas on the way to victory lane.

Gordon had plenty of gas for qualifying for the Coca-Cola 600 and he had plenty of power in his No. 24 Chevrolet in winning the pole. For the fifth straight year, Gordon started first in Winston Cup racing's longest event. That tied David Pearson's record for consecutive 600 poles, and helped ease some of the disappointment his race team felt since The Winston.

THE STREAK

From June 28 at the Sears Point road course to September 9, 1998, at Darlington, the Rainbow Warriors dominated the Winston Cup Series like few have, especially in NASCAR's modern era. Gordon won seven of nine races during the stretch and finished third at New Hampshire and fifth at Bristol. Both road course events, another Brickyard 400 at Indianapolis, and the Southern 500 at Darlington for the fourth straight time were also among the victories.

As if that wasn't enough Gordon won three of the last four races of the year, including the season-ending NAPA 500 at Atlanta to register his 13th victory of the year. That tied Richard Petty for the modern NASCAR record of most wins in a season. Gordon also tied the Winston Cup record for consecutive victories with four and became the first driver in NASCAR history to win as many as 10 races for three years in a row. He won the No Bull $5 million bonus from RJ Reynolds for the second straight time with his victory at Darlington.

Gordon won the 1999 Daytona 500 to open defense of his title and won six more races dur-

ing the year, including both road course races again and back-to-back victories at Martinsville and Charlotte in October. Dale Jarrett had finished second to Gordon in 1997 and third in 1998 but broke through in 1999 to win the championship.

The season finale seemed to sum up Gordon's year. In 1998 at Atlanta Motor Speedway, he wrapped up his third Winston Cup championship in four seasons by winning the NAPA 500 to tie Richard Petty's modern-era record of 13 victories in a season.

In 1999 Gordon's No. 24 Chevrolet went out with a blown engine after 181 laps, giving him a 38th-place finish and leaving him sixth in the points standings.

Gordon still won more races than any other driver and scored his final two wins after Ray Evernham left as his crew chief to start his own team with Dodge backing. After those wins at Martinsville and Charlotte, Gordon finished no better than 10th in the season's final five races. Five members of his pit crew also decided to leave for Jarrett's team in 2000.

In 2000 Gordon fell to ninth in the standings as Bobby Labonte won his first championship. Gordon won at Talladega, Sears Point, and Richmond.

Before the 2000 season had begun, Robbie Loomis was hired to take over as crew chief for Gordon, who stepped up to take on more of a leadership role with his team. And by 2001,

Gordon had 52 Winston Cup victories, three championships, and victories in NASCAR's premier event, the Daytona 500, in 1997 and 1999.

LOSING A FRIEND

The 2001 Daytona 500 saw a lethal crash for seven-time champion Dale Earnhardt. Gordon won the pole the following week and wore a Dale Earnhardt cap for interviews after taking his 34th career pole position.

"He was somebody I respected greatly and I learned a lot from him—more than he ever imagined," Gordon said. "That's why I put this No. 3 hat on and let everybody know we're thinking of Dale. I want to dedicate this to him. It's a great opportunity to let everyone know how much I respected him and how much we're going to miss him."

Gordon regained the form of his championship seasons and won the third race of the year at Las Vegas, then opened June with victories at Dover and Michigan. He led 381 of 400 laps in the former and the latter gave Rick Hendrick his 100th win as a team owner.

In October Gordon dodged wrecks, penalties, and other calamities that cost his rivals dearly to win the inaugural Winston Cup race at Kansas Speedway, the 20th track on which Gordon had gone to victory lane.

At age 30, a fourth Winston Cup championship looked inevitable. Gordon was already one of seven drivers with at least three titles, and on average the other six didn't win their first titles until age 33. Richard Petty and David Pearson were 34 when they won No. 3.

It took Petty 15 years to win four titles, Dale Earnhardt 12.

Gordon didn't win another race in the 2001 season after Kansas, but he still secured his fourth title.

Dale Earnhardt had won his sixth and seventh titles in Gordon's first two full seasons of Winston Cup competition, 1993 and 1994, while Gordon watched and learned.

"He never gave up, never. That guy, it didn't matter whether his car was way off or if he was laps down, he never stopped driving the wheels off of that thing. Every position, every point means something," said Gordon.

"He wanted to be that eight-time Winston Cup champion and he got seven of them because he knew what he was doing. Winning races is great, but there's nothing better than winning championships."

Y O U N G   G U N S

The Future

Gordon's success rate in NASCAR's top series almost defies anyone's belief. His 58 victories lead all active drivers, and he got his first win at 22, much younger than Bobby Labonte (31), Dale Jarrett (34), Rusty Wallace (29), and Bill Elliott (28).

"A lot of the guys didn't get to Winston Cup until later than I did," Gordon said. "I was able to get with a top organization from the start and that allowed me to be successful at a lot younger age."

If Gordon keeps his pace and wins four more titles in the next nine seasons, he'll get a record eighth championship in 2010 with his 40th birthday still a season away. But he's not sure he or anybody else can reach that feat.

"They're wearing us out," he said. "The schedule is so intense, and it's not just 36 races. It's that plus everything that comes along with having a $15-million-per-year sponsor. These guys are paying a lot of money and they expect to get something in return for their investment, and I expect them to.

"When you're a champion, opportunities come along that are hard to turn down. . . . Those things will shorten how long you're going to race."

Or have to race, he says.

"If I were to stop today, I would have to change my lifestyle. That shouldn't be the determining factor, but if there comes a day when you're not having fun and the desire is

not there and you ask if you can give up all of the other stuff, I certainly could.

"As long as I am healthy and competitive and the desire is there I am going to keep racing," Gordon says. "I don't put an age limit on it, but if any one of those things goes away it could stop me sooner."

Gordon's blip—the departure of crew chief Ray Evernham and an ensuing upheaval and retooling of his team at Hendrick Motorsports—didn't come until after his third title, and it lasted only two seasons. So far, Gordon has avoided major injuries that are always a risk for a Winston Cup driver, and his

24

emotional batteries seem recharged by his new leadership role in the team.

He has a lifetime contract with Hendrick Motorsports and is part owner in the No. 48 team with young phenom Jimmie Johnson as driver. In 2002 Johnson became only the third rookie ever to win a pole for the Daytona 500.

"I admire Jeff so much," said Tony Stewart, who finished second in the 2001 standings and looms as a possible rival to Gordon's future success. "He gets it right every time. No matter the situation, it seems like he handles it exactly the right way."

Like a champion.

KEVIN HARVICK

Black Sunday at Daytona

There was no question that Kevin Harvick showed he had the talent needed to make it as a star in the NASCAR Winston Cup Series. What nobody expected, however, was the tragic situation that led to him being called up to drive at the Winston Cup level in 2001: the death of seven-time champion Dale Earnhardt.

At that time, team owner Richard Childress was faced with a tough situation. Would he put another driver in the famed black No. 3 GM Goodwrench Chevrolet, or would the loss of one of his best friends be enough to cause him to decide to walk away from the sport? Those were questions that Childress faced after returning from the Daytona 500.

"That whole night, once I got home, I never slept. I just laid there and thought," Childress said. "It was an emotional deal for me and my wife. I got up the next morning saying, 'I don't even want to go to a race.'"

In those dark and emotional hours that followed, Childress did a little soul searching and thought about what Earnhardt would want him to do. He decided that Earnhardt would have wanted the show to go on, even though it might be painful. That's exactly what Childress decided to do after discussions with longtime employees Bobby Hutchens and Kevin Hamlin.

"Bobby and Kevin Hamlin both said, 'You know what Dale would want you to do and we have got to do it,'" Childress said. "That's all it

took for them to tell me what Dale would want me to do. I did exactly that and I know that is what Dale would have wanted."

With the Winston Cup tour set to return to action the following week in Rockingham, it was announced that Harvick would fill the seat of one of the greatest drivers in NASCAR history. It would be Earnhardt's car, but it was still too painful for everybody involved to see his old car number and paint scheme on the track. Instead of the familiar black No. 3, Harvick wanted to establish his own identity—so he switched numbers to No. 29 and went with a silver car with a hint of black.

"This is still Dale's team," Harvick said. "This is still what he built, and we just wanted to do what he would have wanted us to do after he decided to quit, and that's run it competitively."

Before he accepted the ride, Harvick wanted to make it well known that there was no way he could ever fill the shoes of Earnhardt.

"I'll do whatever it takes for this race team," Harvick told Childress. "You tell me what you want me to do, I'll go out and do it,

and I'll do my best. But I can't come in here and replace Dale Earnhardt. I'll come in as Kevin Harvick and drive the car for you."

Though not by design, Harvick would go on to experience one of the most successful rookie seasons in Winston Cup history. In addition to running his first season in Winston Cup, Harvick also competed in the Busch Series and won the championship in a car owned by Childress. Running one of the divisions is considered a daunting task, but Harvick pulled off the feat in convincing fashion.

Harvick not only won the championship in the Busch Series but also finished a remarkable ninth in the Winston Cup standings and picked up two victories despite missing the 2001 season opener at Daytona.

Many thought there was no way Harvick could race and be competitive in both divisions, which made him all the more hungry to prove those critics wrong.

"I think it will take four to five years for all of the guys who were involved with our team to fully realize what we did," Harvick said. "It was

a big deal. We did something 99 people out of 100 didn't think we could do. It was cool."

Childress realizes that Harvick performed extraordinarily under extremely tough conditions.

"Kevin Harvick is the real deal," said Childress, with whom Earnhardt won six of his record-tying seven Winston Cup titles. "I have been in this sport 30-some years and I've seen some of the greats come along. I think Kevin has everything he needs to be one of the greats."

There has been a big difference in the 2002 Winston Cup season compared to the previous year, not only for Harvick but also for teammates Jeff Green and Robby Gordon. Harvick struggled rather badly through the first half of the season, prompting Childress to switch the entire crews between Harvick and Gordon. The move paid dividends when Harvick won the Tropicana 400 at Chicagoland Speedway in July, a week after winning his first career pole for the Pepsi 400 at Daytona.

While winning the 2002 championship was out of the picture because of the early season struggles, many of the sport's veterans felt that the class Harvick showed so early in his career is going to lead to big things in the future.

"I hope everybody understands what he's doing and the accomplishments he has had and the mark he's made," said 1999 Winston Cup champion Dale Jarrett. "He's a remarkable young man and a tremendous talent. There are very few people, if anybody, who could take on what he has taken on, especially at the young age he is, and do the job he has done."

Path to Stardom

Kevin Harvick is a native of Bakersfield, California, who has always possessed a love of auto racing. At the tender age of five he began racing go-karts and did a pretty good job, winning seven national titles and two Grand National championships.

At the age of 18, Harvick had started to make others take notice of his talent behind the wheel of a stock car by winning the 1993 Late Model championship at his hometown track of Mesa Marin Raceway. From there it's been a meteoric ride to the top of the NASCAR ranks for Harvick, who has moved up the ladder at a blistering pace.

In 1995 Harvick won top rookie honors in the Featherlite Southwest Series while picking up a victory at Tucson and finishing 11th in the final points championship. He won the 1998 NASCAR Winston West championship and started to become a young talent many of the top team owners were looking to take a chance with.

Harvick would get the chance to prove himself in the NASCAR Craftsman Truck Series in 1999, and while he didn't win a race, he posted a respectable 11 top-10 finishes. When Richard Childress started to look for a Busch Series driver to replace Dale Earnhardt Jr., who was moving up to Winston Cup, Harvick would get the opportunity of a life-time to prove his talent by getting the nod in the No. 2 A. C. Delco Chevrolet in 2000.

Ironically, Childress and Dale Earnhardt used to jokingly argue about which one of them was going to be the first to sign Harvick at the Winston Cup level. In his first full season, Harvick would more than prove himself worthy of the hype, winning three races, two poles, and top rookie honors, and finishing a strong third place in the final standings.

Heading into the 2001 season, Harvick was a man on a mission, determined to win the Busch Series championship. One day after opening the season at Daytona with a second-place finish, everything in the life of Harvick and Richard Childress Racing would be altered with Earnhardt's fatal last-lap crash in the Daytona 500.

Because he would have to split his time between the Winston Cup and Busch Series cars, not everybody in the garage area was sold on Harvick. In fact, many of the Busch Series races were at tracks where the Winston Cup tour doesn't compete, which meant Harvick spent plenty of time in airplanes getting from place to place.

By the time the 2001 season was over, Harvick had competed in 70 races, including one start in the Craftsman Truck Series. His effort in both divisions was impeccable—Winston Cup Rookie of the Year with two victories as well as the Busch Series crown.

In a season of adversity, Harvick shocked the racing world in only his third career start and in one of the most emotional races in Winston Cup history. With the Childress camp as well as the rest of the NASCAR community still in shock over the death of Earnhardt, Harvick would win his first race at Atlanta Motor Speedway in a photo-finish victory over four-time series champion Jeff Gordon.

"What could be better?" Harvick said in victory lane. "That's so much better than going out and leading 400 miles of a 500-mile race to get your first win. To go out there and do it the way we did, like Dale Earnhardt did it a year before, just shows you there is somebody still in our sport watching over us."

To some, it was the start of the healing process. For others, it was emotional because it was the one-year anniversary of an Earnhardt victory at Atlanta in the exact same fashion over Bobby Labonte. To Childress, it was vindication that his desire to stay in racing after the loss of Earnhardt was the right one.

Standing in victory lane—for the first time in 17 years with a driver other than Earnhardt—tears could be seen streaming down the face of Childress and other team members less than a month after the death of "The Intimidator."

"This is unbelievable for everybody," Childress said. "We'll never get over Dale, but this is comforting because we know we are doing what Dale wanted us to do. We know he wanted us to go out and win. We had talked about the day whenever he eventually would decide to retire. He wanted us to put someone in the car that could go out and win. I know he is up there smiling down on us right now. Kevin has given us all the strength to go forward."

Even NASCAR President Mike Helton said Harvick's victory couldn't have come at a more needed time for the sport.

"The biggest thing was it was just great racing, and that's what we strive to do each week," Helton said. "The first thought was for Teresa Earnhardt and Richard and Judy Childress and his entire operation. To be able to celebrate again was a big deal. For Childress to be able to pull from all the strengths that they were able to pull from, to stay on track and be successful, I think that says a lot for the organization, for Kevin Harvick's character and talent, and the legacy of Dale Earnhardt. That is what it's all about."

Harvick would also pick up another Winston Cup win later in the 2001 season in the inaugural race at Chicagoland Speedway, and defended as the race winner in 2002, but nothing will ever come close to his win at Atlanta. It was a script that was heaven sent.

No Fear Here

Even though 2002 is technically Kevin Harvick's first full season at the Winston Cup level due to the fact that he didn't race in 2001's Daytona, don't think for a moment that the Winston-Salem, North Carolina, resident is going through the rookie motions.

As he proved in 2001, Harvick is going to be in contention for race wins and championships. In only a year and a half, he's been through the highs and lows that come along with trying to reach stardom at the Winston Cup level.

Sometimes his enthusiasm and passion for winning have led to problematic encounters with some of his fellow drivers, as well as NASCAR officials. In this sport, any team owner will say it's much easier to have to pull back the reins on drivers than to try to make them go faster and be more aggressive.

"I enjoy racing and some people get worried about getting run into or running into people, but that kind of stuff is going to happen," Harvick said. "There are 43 guys out there and we're all there to race. These sponsors don't spend $10 million to watch us have a nice car show. They want to see us race. I enjoy racing and I enjoy being at the race track. I enjoy competition and I hate to lose, but I think there's a lot of other guys out there that have the same thing in mind and that's why people like this sport so much."

At times, Harvick has been accused of crossing the line. In the fall 2001 race at

Martinsville, while battling for position with Bobby Hamilton, both cars got into a bumping match that left Hamilton steaming mad after the day was over.

"He's just trying to be Dale Earnhardt," Hamilton said. "Earnhardt knew how to do it and Kevin doesn't. Somebody will black his eyes for him because Earnhardt had earned a lot of respect for everybody. The kid's got a ton of talent and he's going to do a lot for NASCAR. That is what Richard Childress wanted and that's what he's got. You just don't go hiring another Dale Earnhardt. I think he needs to do what he's capable of doing and that's it. He'll still be fine, but he'll never be what Earnhardt was."

Harvick, with a smile, shrugged the comments off before walking away.

"It's an eye for an eye, and that's the way I race," he said.

Earlier in 2002 at Bristol, a longtime feud between Harvick and Greg Biffle spilled over after the race into near fisticuffs between the two drivers. Harvick was upset and felt that he had been intentionally wrecked. He made it known on national television that he would be waiting for Biffle when the race was over. As soon as Biffle started his postrace interview,

35

Harvick jumped over his car and a heated conversation ensued.

As a result of his actions, Harvick was fined and placed on probation by NASCAR. Only two weeks later at Martinsville, Harvick was once again in trouble as a result of intentionally spinning out Coy Gibbs in a Craftsman Truck race after an earlier racing incident. After being ordered to bring his truck in for a penalty, Harvick parked it at the back door of the NASCAR trailer in mocking fashion.

He ended up getting tagged with the worst penalty of his career when he was "parked" by NASCAR officials for the following day's Winston Cup race at the Virginia short track and not allowed to race. At that point, Harvick was going through a tough season that was getting even worse.

In 2001 Harvick was battling to finish in the top 10 in points, while just before the 2002 season's halfway point he was trying to break into the top 30.

"It stunk sitting at home watching that race on television, because I knew I was supposed to be a part of it," Harvick said. "That makes you think about a lot of things and makes you realize a lot of things. I talked to a lot of people. You come to a fork in the road where you can listen and try to understand how the sport works better or you can be stubborn and not accept anything.

"The top echelon of this sport has been the most supportive. They have been there for me with advice. The ones who are voicing their opinion don't really hold that much credibility to me. The people who've called me or come to me with support are the ones I need to listen to, the ones who've been champions and won races in our sport."

In all likelihood, the Martinsville penalty will probably make Harvick a much smarter and more mature driver in the future—which could be a scary thought.

Thrown to the Wolves

In Winston Cup racing, young drivers quickly find the need to surround themselves with quality teams and they often seek advice from their fellow competitors in order to gain experience. Kevin Harvick was no different just because he was thrown into a championship-caliber team from the very beginning of his Winston Cup career.

One of the most important people in Harvick's rise to the top of the sport has been Richard Childress. A longtime veteran of the sport, Childress started out as a driver himself for seven years without a victory before moving over to the role as a team owner.

"My biggest help personally has been Richard," Harvick said. "He's taken me under his wing and before I get somewhere, he'll give me a heads-up on what I need to know—whether it's the press, the fans, or whatever. We're spending a lot of time together and we're communicating well.

"The best thing about our relationship is that if I think something is wrong, I can go to him and ask to change something and I think he respects that. And he's always the first person to tell me if I need to change something. That's the kind of one-on-one relationship that we need to have, and that's what we've got."

Childress has been through good times and bad in the sport, which played a factor when Harvick and his two other race teams got off to such a slow start in 2002. Because of those

struggles, soon rumors began to surface surrounding Harvick's future with RCR and the No. 29 team.

Displeased with the lack of performance not only from the Harvick camp but also from the No. 31 Robby Gordon team, Childress announced a major overhaul in late May. The entire No. 29 team and crew chief Kevin Hamlin moved to Gordon's team while crew chief Gil Martin and crew were teamed with Harvick.

Childress wasn't throwing in the towel with Harvick or Gordon; he just wanted his racing empire to get back to its winning ways.

"I don't know if it was just chemistry or that things just weren't working," Childress said. "There are three kinds of people in the world. There are people that watch things happen, people that make things happen, and people that wonder what the heck happened. Last year was a tough and trying year. I could see some problems the last eight or nine races with the No. 29 car.

"We weren't performing like I felt we should. Kevin was running for the Busch championship and I felt that once we got that and the winter behind us, things would get better. But I didn't see improvement and it was time to change."

Harvick defends the reasoning behind Childress' decision.

"I'm here to stay," Harvick said, officially deflating the rumors that he would be headed elsewhere. "So many people were frustrated with me and didn't understand anything about me. Not once was I ever asked if Richard Childress was mad at me or if I was mad at him. Nobody ever had the nerve to ask me. I have never raised my voice to Richard or ever had him raise his voice to me. We have never ended a conversation and not been on the same page. We were hearing all the crazy rumors about fussing and fighting here. At RCR, there are three teams and we are all in this together."

Less than two months after the crew swap, Harvick took the No. 29 GM Goodwrench Chevrolet to victory lane at Chicagoland Speedway. It was the first win of the season for the Childress teams.

"We're just glad to defend anything at this point," Harvick joked when asked about being the only driver to have won a Winston Cup race in two years of racing at the Chicago track. "The momentum that has been building and the chemistry between myself and Gil and all the guys is really strong. There are a lot of guys like me that haven't won a lot of races.

We're all hungry to win races and hungry to prove everybody wrong. I think we've accomplished all those goals and it's going to be fast forward from here."

Of course, another important part of Harvick's life is the personal side. Like they say, behind every man is a strong woman. For Harvick, that special lady is the former DeLana Linville, whom he married in 2001 in Las Vegas only two days after his first Winston Cup start at North Carolina Speedway in Rockingham.

DeLana Harvick was not new to the racing game. She had worked with former Busch Series champion Randy LaJoie as his press agent. Her husband is the first to give her credit for helping him get through one of the toughest schedules in NASCAR history.

"We had the unfortunate circumstance with Dale and we got thrown in the middle of the fire, I guess you could say," Harvick said. "We got married, then I won at Atlanta, and we thought it was going to calm back down. I've learned that I can only do so much. We just need to keep our feet on the ground."

Bridges to Cross

Considering what Kevin Harvick accomplished as a rookie at NASCAR's top level, many people thought he might very well be a contender in the 2002 Winston Cup championship race.

But from early in the season, it became all too evident that this would not be the year. There was clearly more work to be done in the second half of the season if the team wanted to get back to the top and be a consistent threat every weekend to win races and eventually a Winston Cup championship.

That, however, was highly unlikely to take place by the end of the 2002 season.

There were early distractions within the RCR organization, such as moving from the

old and smaller buildings that were used in Earnhardt's glory days into a more modern facility just across the street in rural Welcome, North Carolina. Another change was the fact that the operation went from a two-car along with Robby Gordon to a multicar team with the addition of Jeff Green in the No. 30 America Online Chevrolet.

According to Harvick, trying to keep one car up toward the front, much less three, is a tall task for any team owner.

"There are a lot of different scenarios that you can point at," Harvick said of 2002's struggles for all three of Childress' teams. "Whether it's right or wrong, nobody knows. To start a third team, that's all where it starts, because we didn't do anything different from the off-season. When you start a third team, you have to worry about how many cars and motors are needed. We started off at Daytona with a wreck and it's just been one thing after another.

"We went into the season with high hopes, but we had all these different circumstances that were going on. That's not to say that everybody hasn't been working hard because everybody has worked their guts out since the season ended last year. We just haven't had the time to go do the things that we needed to do—whether that's the reason or not. We've got this good stuff that we raced last year and we thought we'd made it better. It's just all these things add up, piles just keep getting bigger, and we've just now started to knock the piles back down."

Harvick pulled a rather large upset with his July victory at Chicago, a race in which very few saw him as a serious threat, considering his performance going into it. After the win at the season's midway point, Harvick moved up to a dismal 28th in the standings, while teammates Gordon sat 24th and Green 22nd.

After being teamed with crew chief Gil Martin, Harvick seemed to turn the corner and was getting better and better with each race.

"When we switched everything around, Gil told me, 'Look, just give me a couple of weeks here and we'll get everything going in the right direction,'" Harvick said. "So as a team and an organization we could see that things were going better by the performance on the track. We weren't getting lapped on the track anymore or finishing bad because we ran bad, we were just having some dumb racing luck. Like I said, we've been really hard on ourselves. Anybody that's not wearing silver and black just doesn't understand what we're thinking or what we need to do. As a team and as a company, RCR and GM Goodwrench as well as all the people that surrounded us knew that everything was going a lot better and there were some positive things that were happening."

Before the win in Chicago, Harvick had only one other top-five finish to his credit. Some look at his one-race suspension at Martinsville as one of the reasons. Make no mistake about it: Harvick deeply regrets putting his team in a rut for his actions in the spring truck race at Martinsville.

"I think the biggest thing I've learned is that through these situations, you have to come back and gain a little bit of respect," Harvick said. "It's not about the fact I can't be aggressive, but it's just that I can't retaliate with my vehicle as a weapon. That's the biggest thing that I learned. We're out there racing and there's going to be a lot of things that happen and you just have to understand those situations and really try to step back and realize what's going on.

"The Martinsville incident really made me realize what was going on, what I needed to do, and what I needed to change and learn. I told everybody from the beginning that the way I drive wasn't going to change. It's just the fact that there are just three or four little things that I did that pushed it over the limit, and I need to take those and learn by them."

Childress has no doubt that Harvick has what it takes to give him his next Winston Cup championship—after Earnhardt delivered six of seven in his tenure with RCR.

"We still have got a lot of hurdles to cross," Childress said. "I wish I could say that everything was uphill from here, but we've got a lot to do. . . . It's going to take a lot of work to get us there, but there are a lot of things in the future that we're working on."

He's an Earnhardt

"Earn-hardt! Earn-hardt! Earn-hardt!"

Thousands of fans at Lowe's Motor Speedway were chanting his name in unison, and Dale Earnhardt Jr. was looking around to see whom they were calling for.

"Earn-hardt! Earn-hardt! Earn-hardt!"

Earnhardt Jr. had heard the chant dozens of times before. He'd sometimes been there when race fans shouted as one in praise of his father, seven-time NASCAR Winston Cup champion Dale Earnhardt.

This time, though, things were different.

The date was May 20, 2000, and minutes earlier The Winston all-star race had just wrapped up in thrilling fashion. An Earnhardt had roared from the back of the pack in the

final eight laps, taking the checkered flag in an event that had, from its inception, seemed to be custom-designed to fit the Earnhardt driving style.

The fans kept on chanting, and Earnhardt Jr. kept on looking around—even though he knew they were cheering for him.

"It was kind of funny for me to stand there and hear people cheering, 'Earn-hardt! Earn-hardt! Earn-hardt!' when I'm the only Earnhardt standing up there," Earnhardt Jr. would say that night, soon after becoming the first Winston Cup rookie to win The Winston. "That was kind of weird."

Over the ensuing few years, Earnhardt Jr. would become more comfortable with the

cheers. Tragically, he would also soon begin shouldering more of the burden of carrying the family name into NASCAR's future than anyone could have ever imagined on that night.

Growing up an Earnhardt isn't the easiest thing in the world anyway. Being Dale Earnhardt Jr. is especially tough because the original was, well, an absolute, one-of-a-kind original.

Dale Earnhardt grew up as the son of a famous race car driver, too. His father, Ralph, was one of the greatest short-track racers to ever turn a steering wheel, and his son idolized him. Dale would wake up in the morning after Ralph had raced on some dirt track the night before and run out to look at the car. He could almost always tell how things had gone with one look—if the car was anywhere close to being in one piece, Ralph had most likely brought home a little money from the track.

Dale wanted to be just like his father, but Ralph wanted his son to get at least a high school education. Ralph knew how hard it could be to make a decent living driving a race car, and wanted Dale to have a fighting chance in life if that didn't work out for him. Dale, though, was in a big hurry to start racing and wouldn't listen to Ralph. Dale quit school and Ralph didn't like it one bit.

Dale and Ralph had patched things up before Ralph died of a heart attack at age 45, and as the years passed Dale learned more and more each day just how smart his father had really been.

"I should have listened to my dad better," Earnhardt said. "That's the main lesson in life. Everything he told me came out to be true. Why did I not believe him? I wish I'd have listened better to the basic things he taught me.

"I've told Dale Jr. the same thing. I said, 'You're not going to believe me or listen to me,

but this is what I learned from my dad and it all came true.' I'm giving him advice the best I can."

Over the years, though, it seemed Earnhardt Jr. wasn't listening at all to his one-of-a-kind dad. But by the time he'd made it to Winston Cup, NASCAR's top circuit, it was apparent to anyone paying attention that, at least when it came to racing, Earnhardt Jr. had learned his lessons well.

His father had tied Richard Petty's all-time record by winning seven championships. He'd won every major race in the sport, completing the resume with an emotional victory in the 1998 Daytona 500, and had turned his "Intimidator" image into a public persona and a marketing bonanza.

Earnhardt Jr. has his father's name. In his first three seasons in Winston Cup racing, he

has also shown that he has at least some of his father's skills, especially in solving the mysteries of racing at Daytona and Talladega, the sport's two biggest tracks.

He is not, however, his father.

Earnhardt wore dark sunglasses and hung out with country musicians. Earnhardt Jr. wears his baseball caps backward and dresses in baggy blue jeans and T-shirts like some of the musicians in the rock 'n' roll bands whose music he loves. Earnhardt Jr. surfs the Internet, while the only computer Earnhardt ever mastered was the one that gave him an unmatched seat-of-the-pants feel while driving a race car.

As different as they could be, though, there are also striking similarities. Foremost among those is how Earnhardt Sr. and Earnhardt Jr. both represent a bridge across two distinct eras in what is now America's fastest growing sport.

Earnhardt started his career on the red-clay dirt tracks in the Carolinas, the tracks where Ralph Earnhardt raced well enough to earn a spot among the 50 greatest drivers in NASCAR history. Over the course of his career, he helped propel stock car racing from those roots into the mainstream of America's professional sports psyche, becoming in fact its most recognizable icon.

Earnhardt Jr. stepped into NASCAR's elite just as the sport was beginning to climb its next mountain, becoming a star just as Winston Cup racing moved from cable to network television and just as his father's generation of superstars was heading into its final years of competitive racing. NASCAR was going nationwide, expanding its appeal to a younger, hipper audience.

So far, he has been up to the challenge. Earnhardt Jr. is, perhaps, the closest thing stock-car racing has ever had to a true rock star. And he's one heck of a race car driver, too.

As his father once said, "He's an Earnhardt."

A Legend in the Making

Dale Earnhardt Jr. was born October 10, 1974, in Kannapolis, the small North Carolina textile-mill town where his grandfather and father had both put down the family's roots.

His mother, Brenda, was Dale Earnhardt's second wife and is also the mother of Earnhardt Jr.'s older sister, Kelley. His half-brother, Kerry, was born five years earlier.

Both of Earnhardt's first two marriages ended in divorce, in part because of the demands placed upon a young man trying to balance supporting a family with the cost of pursuing a career in auto racing.

Earnhardt Jr. lived with his mother until just after he started school, but as his father began to enjoy success in Winston Cup in the early eighties, Earnhardt regained custody of Kelley and Earnhardt Jr.

Earnhardt Sr. had quit school after the ninth grade to join racing, a decision that angered his father, Ralph, and Earnhardt grew to regret both his decision to leave school and the rift it caused between himself and his father. He made it clear to his children that he expected them to get their high school diplomas.

Earnhardt Jr. did that, graduating from Mooresville High in 1992, where he played soccer as well, then spent two years studying at a trade school before getting a job at his father's Chevrolet dealership in Newton, North Carolina. Earnhardt Jr. changed oil,

hammered out dents, and did whatever he was asked to do to help out.

Things were not always perfect between Earnhardt Jr. and his dad. Earnhardt Jr. spent the seventh and eighth grades at Oak Hill Military Academy in Greensboro in the hope that it would curb his rambunctious side. He also would later say he resented the fact that his father, who'd been the one insisting he complete high school, missed his graduation ceremony because he was off at a race track.

Their common ground, however, was racing.

Earnhardt Jr. had worked at odd jobs around his father's race shop, learning about the family business bit by bit. He eventually built a red Chevrolet Monte Carlo that, at age 17, he began driving in street stock division races at Concord Motorsport Park, not far from Kannapolis.

"If you pay attention, that's where you get good at what you do," Earnhardt Jr. would say later.

He also raced Legends cars at Charlotte Motor Speedway, half-scale replicas of coupes and sedans from the thirties and forties that then sold for about $8,500.

At the Charlotte track in October 1992, the night before his 18th birthday, Earnhardt Jr. scooted onto the infield grass off Turn 4 on the final lap of a 25-lap race and then bumped Hank Jones—a member of his dad's pit crew and the owner of the car Earnhardt Jr. was driving—out of the way to get his first win.

"I reckon that's the way it goes," Earnhardt Jr. said.

He shared a desire to race with his brother and sister, and in 1994 Earnhardt helped each of them get a shot at running in the late model division on one of the short tracks around the Carolinas. Kerry would run at Hickory Motor Speedway, the historic track where his dad and grandfather had cut their competitive teeth, while Kelley was running at Caraway Speedway in Asheboro and at Concord. Earnhardt Jr., meanwhile, would spend the year chasing the track championship at Myrtle Beach Speedway in South Carolina.

Kelley, who was then a senior at UNC-Charlotte, would eventually give up racing while Kerry continued trying to get his career on the fast track.

Earnhardt Jr., however, was on his way. He didn't dominate at the Myrtle Beach track, but as he continued to learn more and more about his race cars he was also having the time of his life. He raced with a group of guys he considered his friends and spent time with them on

South Carolina's "Grand Strand" when they weren't at the track.

Things would begin to get more serious soon enough, however. He made his first career start in NASCAR's Busch Series when it visited Myrtle Beach on June 22, 1996, finishing 14th.

It's hard for a race car driver named Earnhardt to fly under the radar for long. People began to take notice of the young man who'd so far managed to quietly gain experience, confidence, and—perhaps most critically—his father's trust.

In 1997 Dale Earnhardt Incorporated put a driver from New York state named Steve Park into a car in the Grand National series. Park won Rookie-of-the-Year honors in that series and when Earnhardt Sr. decided that DEI was ready to make the leap into full-time Winston Cup competition the following season, he decided Park was the driver to do it with.

That left an opening in the Busch Series team's ride, an opening that Earnhardt decided his younger son was ready to fill.

Earnhardt Jr.'s career in NASCAR's big time was about to get the green flag.

Highs and Lows

Earnhardt Jr. dipped his toes into the ocean of NASCAR's Busch Series in 1996 and 1997. In 1998, he waded right in.

His rookie season began at Daytona in February, and he qualified third fastest for the NAPA 300. Considering how famous his father had made that No. 3, it seemed like a good omen.

Perhaps not.

He ran in the top five until an early pit stop, when he came in too fast and slid past his pit stall. His jack man had to jump and roll across the hood to avoid being run over, and when Earnhardt Jr. tried to back into position he tore the drive shaft out of his Chevrolet.

Earnhardt Jr. lost nearly 20 laps as his team made repairs, but his troubles weren't over.

Later in the race, Earnhardt Jr.'s Chevy got tapped from behind on the backstretch by Dick Trickle's car. Earnhardt Jr.'s car then rose into the air and began twisting, landing on Trickle's car before coming to rest against the inside guardrail.

Earnhardt Jr. carried that momentum to Texas Motor Speedway the next time out, and with one lap to go in the Coca-Cola 300 he was right on leader Joe Nemechek's back bumper.

Coming off Turn 4, Earnhardt Jr. used his fresher tires to dive to the inside of Nemechek. Just past the white flag, Earnhardt Jr. got the lead. Elliott Sadler chased the new leader hard on the final lap and got within a car length, but couldn't deny Earnhardt Jr. his first career Busch Series victory.

His father, who'd been coaching Earnhardt Jr. over the radio, was there when the winner pulled into victory lane. They exchanged hugs before Earnhardt Jr. got out of his car.

"That was pretty awesome, wasn't it?" Earnhardt said.

After wrecking three times in a four-race stretch later that spring, Earnhardt Jr. won again at Dover at the end of May. He won again at Milwaukee in July, leading 208 of 250 laps, then took the points lead from Matt Kenseth with another dominant win at California Speedway two weeks later. After getting a penalty for a bumping incident at South Boston, Virginia, the next weekend, he won again at Indianapolis Raceway Park. He led 236 of 250 laps and held off Winston Cup

stars Jimmy Spencer and Jeff Burton to win again at Richmond, solidifying his points lead.

In October, in the 28th of the season's 31 races, Earnhardt Jr. won again at Gateway near St. Louis and padded his lead to 102 points. When he got to Homestead-Miami Speedway for the season's final race, all he had to do was take the green flag to clinch his first Busch Series title. He wrecked in practice and blew an engine in the race, finishing 42nd. It didn't matter. He held off Kenseth by 48 points and brought home a championship for his father's race team.

Daytona had provided a rough start for his rookie season, and things didn't go much better in his sophomore season. Earnhardt Jr. wrecked in his first start in the International Race of

Champions, a race his father won, then crashed his primary car in the final Busch Series practice session. He then wrecked the backup car in the season's first race the following day.

It would be a while before things got better. Earnhardt Jr. tried to keep his mind on racing the Busch car as the days began to count down toward his first Winston Cup start, but there were things even an Earnhardt couldn't control.

His debut was planned for the Coca-Cola 600 at Lowe's Motor Speedway in Charlotte, basically a home game for the Kannapolis native, at the end of May. As he raced through the spring without much success, he couldn't keep from looking ahead toward that date, one that everyone around him was making into such a big deal.

Earnhardt Jr. handled the pressure. He qualified eighth fastest, matching the car number on the side of his Chevrolet Monte Carlo, and finished three laps down to winner Jeff Burton in 16th position.

With the Cup debut behind him, it was as though Earnhardt Jr. had shed a burden. The next weekend, he got his first Busch Series victory of the 1999 season and passed Matt Kenseth for the points lead. He won again the next weekend at South Boston, Virginia, then made it three straight on the road course at Watkins Glen, New York.

During that stretch of racing in June, he also lived out the next chapter of his dreams of racing against his father. In the third IROC race of the season at Michigan Speedway, Earnhardt Jr. came off Turn 4 on the final lap on the outside of his father, racing him for the victory. They traded bumps through the final stretch, with Earnhardt holding on to win by less than two feet.

Before 1999 ended, Earnhardt Jr. had won six Busch races and clinched the championship at Phoenix with one race to go.

Expectations were unquestionably high for his rookie season in Winston Cup. Earnhardt Jr. and Matt Kenseth, who'd battled for two seasons in the Busch Series, were moving up together. Tony Stewart, who'd dazzled the Winston Cup circuit with three wins as a rookie in 1999, predicted the 2000 rookies would quickly make people forget about what he'd accomplished in his first season.

But Earnhardt Jr. didn't win the Daytona 500 to start his rookie season. Then he started second at Atlanta and led the race, but his No. 8 Chevrolet shot suddenly up into the wall. He finished 29th in a race his father won in a side-by-side finish with Bobby Labonte, giving Earnhardt his 75th career win.

Earnhardt Jr. started 10th at Darlington and wrecked again, finishing 40th. He wrecked again at Bristol the next weekend. There were expla-

nations for those wrecks—a cut brake fluid line leaking at Atlanta, a stripped axle at Darlington—but it was still hard for him not to wonder if, perhaps, he might be in over his head. Had he tried to make the move to Cup too soon?

His father, his team, his friends, and just about anybody else he talked to told him no. Their confidence helped keep him from getting down on himself. So, too, did his consistently good qualifying efforts. When he qualified fourth for the DirecTV 500 at Texas Motor Speedway, it was the seventh straight race he'd started in the first six rows.

Earnhardt Jr. had earned his first career Busch Series win at Texas, so he knew the potential was there for a good day. He was in the lead by Lap 17 and at one point later in the race pulled away to lead by more than six seconds over his nearest challenger. At times, he wondered if his car was really that good, or whether other drivers were just waiting to show all their cards.

In the second half of the race, several cars tried two-tire changes on pit stops to gain track position. Tony Eury Sr. stayed with his strategy all day long, however, changing four tires and keeping his driver calm. On Lap 282, Earnhardt Jr. passed DEI teammate Steve Park for the lead and never gave it up again. He pulled away and took the checkered flag nearly six seconds ahead of second-place Jeff Burton.

"Wooooooooooooooooooo!" Earnhardt Jr. screamed over the radio after winning in just his 12th career start.

The incredible moments would keep on coming.

At Richmond in early May, he survived a pit-road bump with Stewart late in the race and went on to pass Earnhardt for the lead with 31 laps to go on his way to his second win.

In the days before The Winston at Charlotte, Lowe's Motor Speedway's president, H. A. "Humpy" Wheeler, who'd known Earnhardt Jr. since he was just a boy, predicted that the sport's hot young star would win the all-star race. Earnhardt didn't like the pick at all, telling Wheeler he was putting too much pressure on the rookie.

"But Dale," Wheeler said, "I think he's going to win!"

And he did, giving him a chance to really celebrate with his father.

Earnhardt Jr. and his team never did find the magic again that year, however, and an inconsistent performance in the season's second half allowed Kenseth, who got his first win at Charlotte the weekend after Earnhardt Jr.'s win in The Winston, to win Winston Cup Rookie-of-the-Year honors.

The late-season dip bothered Earnhardt Jr. He and his crew sometimes found themselves pointing fingers at one another, arguing about who was to blame for the problems instead of figuring out how to fix them.

When the season ended, however, they sat back and looked at what they'd done. They'd won two races plus The Winston and had earned more than $2.8 million. Despite the problems they'd finished 16th in points, certainly respectable if not up to the team's lofty expectations.

Most important, however, the team had established a firm foothold for itself in NASCAR's top division, building on its success from the Busch Series. Earnhardt Jr. was already among the most popular drivers in the sport, and the promise he showed fueled his fame.

On February 19, 2001, on the final lap of the Daytona 500, Earnhardt Sr. hit the Turn 4 wall just as Earnhardt Jr. was chasing DEI teammate Michael Waltrip under the checkered flag. It was Waltrip's first victory in a Winston Cup points race in his first race for DEI, and it should have been a happy day for the Earnhardt team and for the family.

But as the postrace festivities began, race fans began to notice that something was very wrong down on the bottom of the high-banked fourth turn at the track where Earnhardt had won more races than any other driver in history. Emergency workers were scrambling around the black No. 3 Chevrolet, fighting a desperate battle. Earnhardt Jr. climbed out of his car and began running in that direction, sensing that something was terribly, terribly wrong.

Earnhardt's car had broken loose between Turns 3 and 4, shooting up the track toward the outside wall. An eye blink before it hit the wall, the No. 3 Monte Carlo was hit in the side by Ken Schrader's Pontiac, turning it slightly so that the car hit the concrete barrier at an extremely critical angle. All of the forces in the high-speed crash were working together in the worst possible way.

When Earnhardt's car finally came to rest, Schrader's stopped nearby. Schrader jumped out and went to help his fellow driver. He looked inside the No. 3 Chevrolet and quickly began motioning for the ambulance crews to come quickly.

And then he turned away.

The medical crews began working on Earnhardt within a few seconds, and continued their efforts as he was taken from the track and to a hospital just down International Speedway Boulevard. Their efforts to revive him were futile, however.

"I thought he was Superman," Earnhardt Jr. would later say about his father. "I thought he was invincible."

Dale Earnhardt, one of the greatest drivers in NASCAR history, had suffered a basal skull fracture. The blow to his head had been instantly fatal.

The Future

Emotional victories became a Dale Earnhardt Jr. specialty in 2001. After his incredible win at Daytona in July, he next visited victory lane in September at Dover, less than two weeks after the September 11 terrorist attacks on America. In October at Talladega, Earnhardt Jr. won again, furthering the Earnhardt family's rich history in restrictor-plate racing.

Earnhardt Jr. finished his second season eighth in the final standings, eight spots better than he'd done as a rookie. He marched into 2002 looking forward to continuing that improvement and building on the foundation he'd put down in those sometimes difficult first two seasons.

He started the year by winning the season's first Busch Series race at Daytona. He finished second in the Bud Shootout and seemed to have a car strong enough to win the Daytona 500 before problems ended that dream.

Earnhardt Jr. did get his sixth career win at Talladega. He also won over even more fans in The Winston all-star race at Charlotte when he backed off rookie Ryan Newman's car. When Newman got loose less than two laps from the finish after a charging Earnhardt Jr. had nudged him from behind.

Earnhardt Jr. could have wrecked Newman and won the all-star race, but he made the split-second decision not to. Would his hard-charging

father, "The Intimidator," have made the same instinctive decision? Perhaps not.

Earnhardt Jr. brushed aside the praise he got for not taking Newman out, admitting he wasn't sure if he backed off because he didn't want to wreck the rookie or because he thought the rookie was already wrecking. Still, the way Earnhardt Jr. handled the entire affair was yet another sign of how rapidly he had matured.

Image is a funny thing. Some people see Earnhardt Jr. come into the garage wearing blue jeans and a rock band's T-shirt under the perpetually backward baseball cap and see a marketing strategy.

To be certain, Earnhardt Jr. has a public persona that is a little less country and a little more rock 'n' roll. He has been interviewed by Rolling Stone and Playboy magazines and was a presenter at the MTV Movie Awards. He has an endorsement deal with Drakkar Noir, a line of men's fragrances sold in the finest stores.

Earnhardt Jr. personifies a new image for NASCAR racing in many ways. Strong ratings for network TV coverage have propelled NASCAR to a much higher profile nationwide, and Earnhardt Jr.'s popularity is helping to fuel that rise.

That's fine with Earnhardt Jr. He handles the crowds seeking his autograph and pushing for a moment of his time while also dealing with the responsibilities of driving his race car and helping his stepmother, Teresa Earnhardt, guide the future direction of DEI.

He still surfs the Internet and likes to sleep late. He still likes to hang out with his buddies, often in the basement of the house he built on Earnhardt's land, not far from the trailer where he lived just a few years ago. Earnhardt Jr. turned that basement into his own nightclub, complete with floor-to-ceiling speakers, and nicknamed it "Club E." In the past year, however, he's redone things and turned a place where he and his pals used to party into a place where they now more of ten just chill out.

Without question, Earnhardt Jr. is thinking more these days about where he someday wants to be and how he intends to get there.

"I will make some decisions that not everybody might like, but I think people will just have to understand that. . . . I've only got one life; it's not like I can do it over again. So I am going to do it like I want to."

Earnhardt Jr. says the advice his father gave him is more important to him now than ever before. He also has the same fire burning inside. As Earnhardt Jr. gains experience and grows as a racer, he has his sights set on joining his father on the list of the sport's winners.

"My heart has always wanted it, but now I feel it's more of a reality," Earnhardt Jr. said. "I feel like I can be a champion."

KURT BUSCH

Hello, NASCAR

Growing up as a youngster in his hometown of Las Vegas, it would have been easy for Kurt Busch to get distracted and travel down the wrong path.

But Busch would decide that it was in his best interest to avoid a gamble that might lead his career astray. With that the case, he grew up like any normal kid in any normal town.

Though Busch is now one of the top drivers in the NASCAR Winston Cup Series, he really didn't get into racing until his high school days. He is well aware of how far he's come so quickly to make it at the Winston Cup level.

"Every morning I wake up with a smile on my face," Busch said. "I love what I do. It's all I've ever wanted to do. I am just so thankful for the opportunity."

Veteran Winston Cup team owner Jack Roush has always been able to spot a future talent. When Busch and several other young drivers were invited to take part in a 1999 test session for a potential ride in the Craftsman Truck Series, only one stood out after the talent search was done—and that was Busch. As a result of his efforts Busch was rewarded with a multiyear contract with Roush Racing.

"Jack asked me whether I'd be ready to go if the opportunity presented itself," Busch said after signing the contract. "Just the fact that I was considered for the chance was really a

giant confidence boost for me. That was the biggest moment in my life. It made me believe in who I was."

Roush said he knew when he first saw Busch in the 1999 test session that he had a diamond in the rough.

"Kurt Busch has got ice water running through his veins," Roush said. "He is just incredible."

Busch says that if it wasn't for Roush taking the chance on him, he has no idea where or what he would be doing with his life.

"The biggest break of my life came when Jack Roush gave me this opportunity," Busch said. "That's when you know you made it to the big time. But when you make it to the big time, you've got to capitalize on it."

That was exactly what Busch did with his chance.

While he was only hired to drive in the truck series starting with the 2000 season, Busch showed he was capable of bigger and better things in the future. In only his rookie year in the truck series, Busch posted some awesome numbers by the end of the 2000 season. At year's end, he had picked up four victories and four poles to finish an astonishing second in the Craftsman Truck Series championship race. Busch collected four runner-up finishes in 2000, and three of the four races he won came after starting from the pole position. Despite the fact that Busch was racing—and winning—at some tracks that he'd never seen before except on television, he would never fall below seventh in the truck-series point standings throughout the course of the 2000 campaign.

Busch also made his Winston Cup debut in September 2000 at Dover driving a Ford fielded by Roush. He started 10th and finished 18th.

As a result of those efforts Roush catapulted Busch to the Winston Cup ranks for seven of the last eight races to end the 2000 season. Busch's best finish that year came with a 13th-place finish at Lowe's Motor Speedway. Instead of moving him up through the Busch Series ranks—which is considered the normal thing to do to get a young driver extra racing experience, Roush felt as if Busch was ready to go to Winston Cup racing immediately.

Though Busch failed to win top Winston Cup rookie honors in 2001, he did finish second behind fellow first-year driver Kevin Harvick.

"As a rookie I learned a lot," Busch said. "I feel like I did what I was supposed to do, and that was to learn, absorb, and apply lessons learned towards the future. I needed a lot of experience and I got it. I saw a lot of blue sky in some of our efforts in 2001. We were able to have a few good finishes. We showed great potential and matured as a team. That blue sky turned to cloudy gray on occasions, but I knew there was going to be a lot more blue sky on the horizon in 2002."

Sophomore Shuffle

Before the 2002 NASCAR Winston Cup Series season got under way, Kurt Busch was asked what would be the key to a solid sophomore year for him. Busch thought very briefly before answering the question in a single word.

Experience.

Busch would have his wish granted before the start of the 2002 season, when team owner Jack Roush made a massive change between two of his four race teams. The plan was for the entire Busch team from the 2001 campaign to be moved to Mark Martin's team for 2002. In return, Martin's old team and veteran crew chief Jimmy Fennig were moved to speed up Busch's progress.

"I'm really excited about the new opportunity to work with Kurt," said Fennig, who led Martin to 14 victories in five seasons before the pairing went winless in 2001. "Mark and I spent several years working together and winning races, and I'm hopeful that I can add the experience to lead Kurt Busch to many victories."

It would end up being a change that would pay off great dividends for Busch, Martin, and Roush Racing throughout the first half of the 2002 season. At the midway point in 2001 Busch sat 22nd in the points compared to the 2002 season when he was 9th. At the midway point of the 2002 season, Martin was second in the point standings and within striking distance of leader Sterling Marlin, compared to the

same time in 2001, when he was 12th in the standings.

Martin, in fact, was a major advocate of making the switch between the two teams—admitting it was time to make a change in order to be more competitive.

"In my entire racing career I've never had a year where I was not competitive," Martin said. "But last season there were times when we just were not competitive. I've raced for 25 years and it's still hard to say why struggles happen. I was really excited about the 2002 season and the opportunity to work with a fresh group of people. I think that the new lineup brought new ideas to the table and made it really exciting and challenging. Change can be a good thing sometimes. Jimmy Fennig and [car chief] Shawn Parker did a great job for me. I'm sure their experience has been a great asset for Kurt and the No. 97 team."

It was evident from early in the 2002 season that the guidance Fennig was providing Busch was reaping rewards.

"Jimmy Fennig is like a father figure to me," Busch said. "It's great to have the chance to work with somebody as talented as he is. I think we can learn a lot from each other. I have a lot of innovative ideas that I didn't quite know how to develop, but that is where Jimmy has helped. Plus he had a lot of ideas also, and they've proven to be successful. I've already learned a ton from Jimmy. The confidence Jimmy Fennig has in me and all the people on this team has been just unreal. He's a great character and very well-rounded. He's just the mastermind of the Roush Racing crew chiefs.

"It's a great opportunity for the new team to work together and begin a building block. Having Jimmy's leadership and experience has definitely been a help this season, and a step in the right direction. I think that it's made a real impact in terms of his plans and guidance with a rookie such as myself. Jimmy has delivered some great results in the past and it's an honor to work with a crew chief of his stature."

Busch is also quick to credit Roush, who did take something of a gamble in making the changes to his and Martin's teams.

"The amount of people it takes to build a race car and race team to go out there and compete, there are so many individuals I need to mention but there's only one that counts, and that's Jack Roush," Busch said. "It's unbelievable what he's given me and what he's done for me."

It did take a little time to convince Roush that switching the teams was a good idea.

"We made the decision to change crew chiefs for two of our Winston Cup programs after lengthy evaluation of the 2001 season," Roush said. "We feel it's always important to integrate our teams, and this is another example of how each of our drivers and crew chiefs work together. We all have the same goal, and that is to win races and to build championship-caliber teams.

"Our employees were able to see that and realized what we needed to help accomplish that goal. We feel the changes we made will only better our race programs in the future. We're extremely happy with what our crew chiefs have been able to do with their new programs, so we are fortunate that we were able to move them around to achieve that goal."

Breakthrough at Bristol

In less than two full years of Winston Cup racing, Kurt Busch has achieved two major goals that helped him go from a rookie trying to break into the sport to a competitor who is a threat to win on any given weekend.

The first of those two personal goals was achieved during 2001 at Darlington when he won the pole for the Southern 500. The bigger of the two goals, however, came in only the sixth race of the 2002 season when Busch bumped his way past race leader Jimmy Spencer before going on to win the Food City 500 at Bristol to score his first career Winston Cup victory.

"It can't get any better than this," Busch said. "Bristol is a place where just about any-

thing can happen, and for us good pit strategy and a good car led us straight to victory lane. I couldn't be happier about the victory. It's special and very exciting. I'm so excited to finally be able to pick up our first win; it's just an awesome feeling."

Spencer, naturally, saw things from a different perspective and wasn't exactly thrilled with the way Busch took the lead and eventual victory with 55 laps remaining at the high-banked, half-mile track.

"Kurt Busch just smashed right into me, but that's OK because I never forget," Spencer said afterward. "The only thing is when I smash him back, he won't finish the race. I don't know how I saved the car because that was going to be a pretty bad wreck for me. If I get beat fair and square, I'm a big guy and I can handle that. But I can't handle getting smashed into and knocked up and out of the track. You just don't race that way for victories. It's really frustrating."

Despite the controversial bump-and-run, Busch still points to his 2002 victory at Bristol as the greatest win of his career.

"It's so great to get your first win," Busch said. "You wait and wait, and wonder when it's going to happen, and in my case Bristol was the track that I least expected to win on. Jimmy Fennig and the rest of my crew have been working so hard all season in an effort to provide me with the best possible cars, and they have absolutely gone above and beyond. On top of all of it, we are having a great time. Racing is about having fun and performing well, and right now we seem to be doing a lot of both, and I'm looking forward to a continued great 2002 season."

Fennig said it was a relief for Busch and his new team to come together and win a race so quickly.

"It's great," Fennig said. "It's great for this whole team . . . this is not something that one

person can do. Everybody's got to jump in. That's what it's about. We couldn't be happier about winning at Bristol and we have a very exciting 2002 season ahead of us."

While Busch finished second to Harvick in the rookie battle, Jeff Burton's Roush Racing crew chief, Frankie Stoddard, believes Busch has every bit the same talent level and potential as his counterpart showed in 2001.

"I certainly believe that he will eventually be more talented than Kevin Harvick, because he's younger," Stoddard said. "I believe that right now, he's as good as Harvick, given the same amount of experience Harvick has had. Kurt never ran the Busch Series. He learned a lot of these Winston Cup tracks for the first time in 2001. That was the first time he went to a lot of places because all he had raced on was the tracks in the truck series. He did great things in the truck series and then all of a sudden he was moved up into Winston Cup.

"If Kurt Busch had spent two years in the Busch Series, he'd be really setting the world on fire over in Winston Cup. Now that he has had a full year of experience in Winston Cup, I look for him to be strong all year long in 2002."

An Expensive Lesson

Kurt Busch has emerged as a contender that other drivers must deal with on a weekly basis at the Winston Cup level; however, he hasn't made a lot of friends with his fellow competitors due to several questionable actions on his part.

While some of his scraps with other drivers when coming up through the ranks didn't create a lot of attention, Busch quickly found out that every move a Winston Cup driver makes is done under the scrutiny of the public spotlight.

One of the biggest controversies Busch has been through so far in his short Winston Cup career came early in the 2002 season when he bumped Jimmy Spencer out of the lead at Bristol to win his first race at NASCAR's top

level. According to Spencer, there are some drivers out on the track that he can race with side-by-side for 20 laps with no contact and others who don't feel it necessary to show that same respect.

Spencer added that, at least in his opinion, Busch proved that he falls into the latter of the two categories at Bristol.

"You should have a little more respect for the guy leading the race," Spencer explained. "I didn't hit Kurt and I don't think he should have done it to me. I know a lot of drivers that wouldn't have done the same thing and those guys are Winston Cup champions. I really enjoy racing with guys like Jeff Gordon and Tony Stewart. I just look at it as when you

start racing for victories, you had better respect your competitors or it will come back to haunt you pretty quick. Some guys have to learn the hard way."

After his victory, Busch claimed it was late in the race and he was going for the win, and that rubbing and racing are part of the game at Bristol.

"I wasn't going to lay over like a puppy," Busch said after Spencer momentarily took the lead on lap 444 before Busch made contact with his rear bumper and regained the top spot a lap later. "We've all seen Dale Earnhardt slide back underneath people before. We ended up bumping Jimmie [Johnson] a little bit just to rattle his cage."

"Rattle his cage," of course, is the same phrase Earnhardt used after his famous last-lap bump and pass on Terry Labonte in the Bristol night race in August 1999.

While he made it through his rookie season in 2001 without angering a lot of folks, Busch

dealt with more than his share of controversy in 2002.

Less than two months after Bristol, Busch would again find himself in the line of fire for comments he made following The Winston all-star race at Lowe's Motor Speedway. As the field began to spread out in the final 20-lap segment and his chances at the win began to dwindle, Busch tagged and spun out Robby Gordon to bring out a caution in order to bunch the field and get a better chance at the victory.

"We had a shot at the win, and I hated to use Robby to bring out the caution, but I think we needed a yellow there at the end so we could put on a good show," Busch said.

The comments made by Busch created a whirlwind of controversy, and especially didn't sit well with NASCAR officials.

"I think it's safe to say we're looking into it," said Jim Hunter, the manager of communications with NASCAR after hearing that Busch admitted to purposely wrecking another driver.

Many garage-area veterans were shaking their heads in amazement that Busch would make such a claim publicly.

"I am very surprised a guy would admit that he did that," said four-time Winston Cup champion Jeff Gordon. "Whether Kurt meant to do it or not, to joke about or say something about it afterward is probably not the smartest thing to do."

After being fined $10,000 for his postrace comments, Busch conceded that he did the wrong thing.

"This was an expensive lesson," Busch said. "I hope I never get another lesson like this. I chose the wrong words to explain the race."

The fine did little to appease Robby Gordon or his team owner, Richard Childress.

"I will personally kick his [butt] if he ever wrecks one of my cars again and I know he did it on purpose," Childress said. "Write that down in the Bible because it's the gospel. And I can do it. I'm that mad. For him to publicly run his mouth—he's not messing with just anybody."

Robby Gordon was just as angry.

"I'm just disappointed about how immature he is more than anything else," Robby Gordon said. "He said it, so obviously he meant it—he said he used me as a caution. He's just lucky I didn't get hurt or he'd have had some serious problems with my dad and some of my family and the guys on this team. I actually liked Kurt Busch, but now he's off my friends list. I thought he was a pretty bright kid, but now I don't even think he's very bright any more."

The Spoils of Racing

5

I n his short stint on the Winston Cup tour Kurt Busch has left little doubt as to his talent level. It's the ability to take that talent and mix it in with patience that many feel will be his ticket to future stardom at NASCAR's top level.

Controversy in racing isn't always a bad thing as far as ticket sales go—that is, until that adversity takes away from the effort of the driver's team. Some of Busch's actions, such as a July in-car radio tirade against the NASCAR officiating crew at Daytona during the 2002 running of the Pepsi 400, have been immature.

Busch is not alone in his early run-ins with NASCAR officials. Some of the greatest driv-

ers in Winston Cup history have also gone head-to-head with the sanctioning body. That list of drivers includes Richard Petty—who once left NASCAR for drag racing—Cale Yarborough, David Pearson, Junior Johnson (as both an owner and a driver), Bobby Allison, Darrell Waltrip, and the late Dale Earnhardt.

Like all those drivers, Busch knows you have to get on the nerves of a few people to become a winner at the Winston Cup level.

"I want to be the elite," Busch said. "I want to be the best of the best."

A behind-the-scenes look at Busch away from the track shows he's a smart young man with a bright future in NASCAR. Busch is also

learning how to deal with the financial wealth that comes along with being a star in the Winston Cup Series.

At the midway point of the 2002 season—only 60 races into his Winston Cup career—Busch had earned more than $3.5 million in winnings. Naturally most of the winnings go to the team owner, but the drivers also get a hefty portion for their efforts behind the wheel.

Busch is learning to deal with the kind of money that most people can only imagine making. Take into perspective that midway through the 2002 season, Busch had easily surpassed the $1 million mark in winnings.

He's taking a cautious approach toward money.

"I'm not using the M. C. Hammer role model," Busch said, referring to the nineties rap star forced into bankruptcy. "I have an accountant who knows what to do and I'm beginning to get into the financial side in more depth. But it's a different world for me. I'm 24, and I feel like I'm investing like a 35-year-old."

According to Rhett Sinclair, a certified financial planner in Greenville, South Carolina, many young people who face immediate wealth aren't prepared to handle their money wisely.

"They quickly develop a false sense of their wealth," Sinclair said. "They buy big homes, five luxury cars, and lots of jewelry."

The smart thing, said Sinclair, is to do what Busch and others have done.

"They don't make an immediate change in their lifestyle, and they consult with advisers," Sinclair said.

When he was younger, Busch went to college for a year-and-a-half but dropped out to work for the Las Vegas Water District to earn

money so he could pursue his racing dream on the weekends.

"I went to college for Mom, to try to be a pharmacist," Busch said. "But I don't think books were for me."

After Busch caught the eye of team owner Jack Roush following the 1999 test session, he was signed to a contract that paid him about $40,000 annually.

"I would have signed if it said I would make a quarter," Busch said. "That was the biggest moment in my life because it made me believe in who I was. I felt I had failed at college, more or less."

While he is making more money than he ever imagined, Busch really doesn't care to look at it like that.

"I wouldn't call myself rich," Busch said. "I wouldn't know what it meant. For me, it's all about the racing."

Busch knows he has a bright future ahead and he wants to be able to take advantage of the opportunity.

"I know that we're not a car that intimidates people when they see us in the mirror, but I'm working on that," Busch said. "We're working hard to be competitive every week and we are looking stronger every week. We've had a chance to win almost every race so far in 2002, so it's starting to turn around for us."

JIMMIE JOHNSON

Who Is this Guy?

Jimmie Johnson is on the verge of having the most successful rookie season in the history of NASCAR Winston Cup Series racing. Winston Cup racing is not supposed to be an easy sport to break into, but Johnson has sure made it look that way.

Yet his past record in only three Winston Cup races didn't exactly show a great deal of potential as he headed into the 2002 season with a best finish of 25th at Homestead.

Since the No. 48 Lowe's Chevrolet was a new fourth team at Hendrick Motorsports, Johnson absolutely had to make the first four events of the 2002 season or face missing the race. He had no previous car owner points to fall back on and wasn't eligible for a provi-

sional starting position if something went wrong in qualifying.

For Johnson, it proved to be a moot point as he made every race in solid fashion. He also showed a hint of what was to come when he won the pole for the 2002 season-opening Daytona 500. That proved to be even better than his teammate—four-time series champion Jeff Gordon—who qualified just behind Johnson in third place at Daytona. Gordon owns part of Johnson's team, and has been a huge contributor to his new teammate's success.

As it turned out, Johnson bettering Gordon would become the norm through the first half of the 2002 Winston Cup season. While Gordon would struggle through the longest

winless streak since his rookie year, Johnson showed the consistency of a champion. Not only was he running up front, he was also winning races that included victories at California and Dover.

With half the 2002 season down and the final half awaiting, Johnson was well on his way to becoming the most successful rookie in Winston Cup history. Though he led fellow first-year driver Ryan Newman by a 265-237 margin in the battle for Winston Cup Rookie-of-the-Year honors, that was almost an after-thought with Johnson in serious contention to win the Winston Cup championship.

To the shock of almost everybody, Johnson sat third in the point standings and only 89 points behind leader Sterling Marlin. He was also only six points ahead of Gordon, who sat fourth and still very much in contention for a fifth title.

"Jimmie has been outrunning me every weekend," Gordon joked, while noting that Johnson has helped raise the bar at Hendrick Motorsports. "The sport has changed. With the new tires that we have and the amount of downforce that we have, the more aggressive you are in your setups and in your driving, the faster you're going to go and the better you're going to do.

"When you have a young guy like Jimmie who comes into that from the start, knowing he has to drive the wheels off of it and that the car is going to stick, then you get a young crew

chief like Chad Knaus throwing aggressive setups at it, they go that way. We won the championship last year with the setups we had and we didn't want to get too far off those. We're finding ourselves having to push the edge closer to some of the things Jimmie's team has done."

To date, the most successful rookie season in Winston Cup history belongs to Tony Stewart, who scored three victories and finished fourth in the final 1999 standings. In comparison, Johnson had picked up two victories in only 16 career starts while Stewart didn't win until his 25th race. Johnson had picked up three poles, while Stewart had none until September of his rookie season.

Johnson is almost in awe at what he's accomplished so fast in his young career.

"I never ever would have thought we'd have this kind of success," Johnson said. "It's just incredible to have three poles, two wins, and be third in points in just our rookie season as a team."

Newman admitted he was a little envious that Johnson made it to victory lane before he did.

"I was frustrated because I wanted to be the first one to win a race as a rookie this year in the battle but, at the same time, I was happy for him," Newman said. "I think we've got a pretty good relationship where we're happy when each other does well. We want to see each other do well because we've got the best opportunity of lives."

Destiny's Child

Jimmie Johnson didn't travel the path normally taken to reach the Winston Cup Series (although there is no surefire method as to how to reach NASCAR's top level). Being a native of California, Johnson spent his early career racing in off-road trucks on the West Coast and far removed from stock cars.

Five years ago, Johnson is the first to admit, he was basically an unknown commodity to just about everybody in the Winston Cup garage.

"I've worked very hard to get where I am," Johnson said. "I started at the age of five in racing, came from Southern California through motorcycles, off-road truck racing, and just finally got into a stock car four seasons ago."

Johnson's caring and concerned parents had finally arranged for him to race in something with doors and fenders.

"My parents were a little tired of the bruises and broken bones from racing motorcycles, so through their contacts they were able to get me in a car," Johnson explained. "From there I started to race off-road in the Mickey Thompson Stadium Series before I got into ASA racing."

Before moving into the American Speed Association ranks, Johnson had six different kinds of championships under his belt. The ASA division has been a tremendous breeding ground for some of the greatest drivers in Winston Cup history, including Rusty Wallace,

Mark Martin, Ken Schrader, Johnny Benson, and the late Alan Kulwicki.

A short and successful stint in ASA led to a three-race Busch Series opportunity for Johnson in 1998. The following year he competed in five Busch Series races, leading 22 laps and collecting a top-10 finish.

Johnson's first full season in the Busch Series was a successful one. He finished 10th

in the final 2000 point standings despite not winning a race. Like a fine wine that gets better with age, Johnson stepped it up in 2001 while driving for Herzog Motorsports and won his first Busch Series race at Chicago before finishing eighth in the point standings.

People were starting to take notice of Johnson's talent behind the wheel.

"When I was driving in the Busch Series with Herzog Motorsports, it was surprising to me how many people paid attention to the situation I was in," Johnson said. "They knew that I was with a young team. The team was very dedicated and put a lot of money into it, but as important as it is for a driver to have experience, the team I was driving for was a rookie as well."

Johnson's life would start to change later in the 2000 season after he asked for some advice from fellow California native Jeff Gordon. He was told to hold off on making any quick career decisions because Gordon might have an opportunity for him.

"I went to Jeff for some advice in August of 2000 at Michigan," Johnson explained. "People were coming up to me and letting me know they were interested and asking what my obligation was to my Busch team. There was a lot

of stuff going on and I went to Jeff for advice. To my surprise, he was interested and Rick Hendrick was interested in trying a fourth team, and all of a sudden, they were looking at me as being their driver."

Johnson, of course, jumped at the chance to come on board with a new, fourth Hendrick Winston Cup team for the 2002 season.

"I've been pinching myself ever since I signed with this team," Johnson said. "I've got welts all over. If you have that foundation underneath you and take advantage of the resources around you, the sky's the limit. I'm learning fast. I've learned how much more pressure, prestige, and focus there is in Winston Cup racing. It's been a whirlwind for me, but Jeff Gordon and Rick Hendrick wanted to build a team for the future.

"They both wanted to start with a young driver and develop that driver on the skills they have and grow them into a Winston Cup championship – caliber team each week. The situation is we're building a team for the future, with a young team working side-by-side with an experienced team and a veteran driver like Jeff Gordon. The way the whole thing has been set up has given me a forum to grow as a driver and develop."

Teamed with a Champion

When it comes to Winston Cup Series racing, Jimmie Johnson can seemingly do no wrong. Everything the rookie touched throughout the first half of the 2002 season turned to gold.

Johnson obviously has driving talents, but thanks to Jeff Gordon, he also was placed in some very good equipment. Gordon has been around the sport long enough to know that rookie drivers hold their breath for the first month because most don't have past car owner points to fall back on if something goes wrong in qualifying. With that the case, Gordon gave Johnson several of his former race-winning cars to push him over the edge. One of the cars that Gordon gave up was the mount he

won two races with in 2001, and the very same car Johnson drove to his first career Winston Cup victory at California in 2002.

"I guess if I was really struggling and I wanted the car back, I probably could get it," Gordon said with a laugh. "They've built new cars and we've built new cars. They do have some of our older cars. But we feel like every time we build a new car, it's a better car. They have really done a great job with some of the set-ups they put underneath their cars to make them go fast."

While the cars were given to Johnson, it was the job of crew chief Chad Knaus to set up the winning package. Knaus came on board with the Hendrick operation and Gordon's

team, known as "The Rainbow Warriors," before leaving to take over as crew chief for Stacy Compton at Melling Racing.

When the opportunity arose for Knaus to return to Hendrick Motorsports as Johnson's crew chief in 2002, he jumped at the chance. The pairing showed they were going to be a factor early on by winning the pole for the 2002 season-opening Daytona 500, with Johnson becoming only the third rookie in history to earn the top starting sport for the biggest race on the Winston Cup schedule.

"It's hard to believe," Johnson said of the accomplishment. "It really reflects the hard work everybody at Hendrick Motorsports put forth, and it's a great way to start the season."

At California, Knaus gambled on a late pit stop and rewarded his driver with his first win in only 13 Winston Cup starts.

"My hat is off to Chad Knaus," Johnson said following his victory in the 10th race of the 2002 season. "We're both in a similar situation of trying to prove ourselves. He's doing an awesome job and the same with all these guys wearing Lowe's uniforms. This is unbelievable. You always think you have the ability to come out here and be competitive, but you just don't know until the right situation presents itself and you can showcase your talents.

"To be this competitive in Winston Cup racing has been a dream of mine and I just can't believe it has come true. It's just so special to win my first race in my home state and in front of all my friends and family. It's just incredible."

Showing his win at California wasn't a fluke, Johnson picked up his second career victory at Dover and moved up to second in the Winston Cup point standings. That fact led many to feel as if Johnson had a realistic chance—albeit against great odds—to win the Winston Cup title in only his first year on the tour.

Johnson tried his best not to look too far ahead.

"With my inexperience in these cars and this series, I guess we might be a dark horse if anything," Johnson said. "But if we just keep finishing races, the points will take care of itself. We've got a shot at it. Is it realistic? I don't think it's very realistic for a rookie to do that, but crazier things have happened."

Even some of the veterans of the sport have been in awe at what Johnson has done so far.

"Jimmie is driving for the same team that Jeff Gordon is driving for and he's been out-performing a four-time champion," Jeff Burton said. "Man, that's awesome."

Chance of a Lifetime

There have been two key players in Jimmie Johnson's recent racing career that have helped the young driver cross the threshold into stardom at the NASCAR Winston Cup Series level.

One of those people is Jeff Gordon, who wanted to add Johnson as his teammate. The other critical person was team owner Rick Hendrick, who listened to Gordon's praise of Johnson and added him to the Hendrick Motorsports stables for the 2002 season.

With all working together in harmony, Johnson and the entire No. 48 team led by crew chief Chad Knaus have done a masterful job in putting the pieces together to build a championship-caliber team in only half a racing season.

"I'm just blown away," Johnson said. "Coming into the year knowing I would be driving for Rick Hendrick and the way the team was going to be working with Jeff Gordon's team, everybody could see the potential was there. I was just as curious as everybody else. Chad Knaus and I clicked instantly. The resources at Hendrick Motorsports have allowed us to do what we need to do on the track and not worry about anything else. There hasn't been any pressure or stress. We've just worked on communicating and polishing up on our game each week."

Gordon is not only a part owner in Johnson's No. 48 team but also one of his best friends away from the track. In fact, Johnson's victory at California earlier in the year gave Gordon his first win as a car owner.

"Jimmie is just a talent and a smart driver," Gordon said. "We're really thrilled to have him. What a great job they're doing. Plus you've got to give credit to Hendrick Motorsports. That is not to take anything away from the No. 48 team, because they do a great job. They're getting aggressive with the setups and making it work. But they came into an organization that really knows how to put great equipment out there. I told Jimmie that we would put him in top-notch equipment and he's really making it work."

Johnson believes he'd be nowhere close to where he is today without the help of Jeff Gordon.

"Jeff helps me out in more ways than he realizes," Johnson said. "I spend a lot of time studying his data, looking at what he does in the car, and his habits of driving the car. Then I compare them to mine. I've been able to understand what he means when he talks about driving into the corners too hard or picking up the gas early. I've adjusted my style accordingly so that when I go ask him a question, we're talking the same language. It's really kept me in check. They're just simple one-liners. Jeff doesn't realize how much these one-liners mean and what I'm learning from him."

Johnson's two wins and three poles to lead the Hendrick brigade in 2002 made the boss proud that he took the chance on a rookie driver, just like he did with Gordon in 1993.

"I've been very blessed," Hendrick said. "I've been very fortunate, but you have to work hard, have good crews and good chemistry. Jimmie and Chad have proven that. You've got to have confidence and communication for these teams to work, and boy, those two guys have got it."

While the friendship between Gordon and Johnson is relatively new, Hendrick had known Johnson since watching him race with his son, Ricky Hendrick, in the Busch Series. Rick Hendrick would later joke that one of the first times he met Johnson wasn't under the best of circumstances.

"I waited three-and-a-half hours at a race to bring him home," Hendrick said. "Jimmie and my son are good buddies and at a Busch Series race in St. Louis a couple years ago, Ricky fell out of the race and said, 'We can't leave, Dad. Jimmie's going home with us.' On the way home Jimmie started asking questions and he's been like a member of the family every since.

"I remember Jeff happened to be in the Busch Series garage helping Ricky at

Darlington and Jimmie was parked right beside us. Jeff told me that Jimmie got around the place real well, so I asked him how many times he'd been there testing and Jimmie said that was his eighth lap on the track. Jeff and I thought he was such a good talent. It was almost a mirror image of Jeff's deal. We knew Jimmie was a young guy with a lot of talent. When you see them, you just try to take advantage of it. I never dreamed we'd do this well this quickly."

Good Times, Bad Times

With two victories and three pole positions in the first half of the 2002 NASCAR Winston Cup Series season, many race fans might have felt that Jimmie Johnson was becoming too accustomed to winning without going through the normal struggles of a rookie year.

Johnson insisted that was far from the case. He was well aware that what goes up must come down. If he ever doubted that, all he had to do was look to Hendrick Motorsports teammate and four-time series champion Jeff Gordon, who was in the midst of the longest losing streak since his rookie season.

Johnson knows that there are going to be times of struggle. Winston Cup racing is not easy—nor is it supposed to be.

"Right now everything is really clicking," Johnson said. "I wish we could bottle it up and store it for years and just keep doing this forever, but we are going to enjoy the wave while we can."

Johnson admitted he felt the weight of the world on his shoulders as he headed into the 2002 season with a new team that was very capable of big things.

"I felt a lot of pressure coming into this season and driving for Hendrick Motorsports," Johnson said. "Gordon had just won the Winston Cup championship last year. So there was a lot of pressure that I tried to hide. With Rick Hendrick and Jeff Gordon being as laid-back as they are, it helped take some of the pressure off. But there is still pressure.

I think the hurdle and pressure for us is going to be to continue to run up front. We're setting some high expectations now, but when we hit a slump, that's when the pressure is going to be on.

"We're all preparing for it as a team and talking about enjoying the highs while they're here. When the lows come, it will be a character-building opportunity and we'll try to make the most of it. The true test will be when it happens, and that could be the next six races or six years down the road. Everybody goes through it in their career."

Johnson, though, has been through a couple of rough races in 2002 and let a couple of victories slip out of his grasp.

"I had two opportunities—one at Richmond and one at Lowe's in the 600—and I blew it. I can't blame anyone but myself. I wrecked at Richmond and slid through the pits at Charlotte. It's just as easy to lose a race as it is to win one. I found that out late in both of those events."

At Richmond, Johnson clearly had a strong car. He was making a bid for the lead against Jimmy Spencer as he was coming off the third

turn and wrecked. Instead of his second Winston Cup victory, Johnson was left disgusted with a torn-up car and a 31st-place finish.

"There was a bump on the track that I must have caught at the wrong time trying to get underneath Spencer," Johnson said. "I don't think we even touched. I know we were close and racing hard, but it's just a shame that the car turned around on me. I really felt we had the car to beat. I'm just disappointed that I made a mistake that cost us some points and got us torn up. I'm just a little dumbfounded. I really thought we had a shot, but there's nothing I can do about it now."

Probably the hardest luck Johnson has experienced so far at the Winston Cup level happened in May 2002 at Lowe's Motor Speedway in the Coca-Cola 600. Johnson had the entire field at his mercy, leading 223 of the race's 400 laps before a late-race penalty on a pit stop dropped him out of contention and into a seventh-place finish.

"It hurts, but that's how it goes," said a dejected Johnson. "I can't blame anybody but

myself. I was trying to get everything I could on that pit stop and slid about two or three inches too far through my stall and the nose was across the line. We had to back up before we could start our pit stop. The couple of seconds we lost in the pits cost us nine positions on the track.

"On the restart I was stuck back in ninth with the lapped cars on the inside and pretty much doomed. I'm very disappointed. We'll just come back smarter and go to Dover and try to win there."

Johnson and his No. 48 team did just that as he won his second Winston Cup race at Dover the following week to creep even closer to becoming the most successful rookie driver in history.

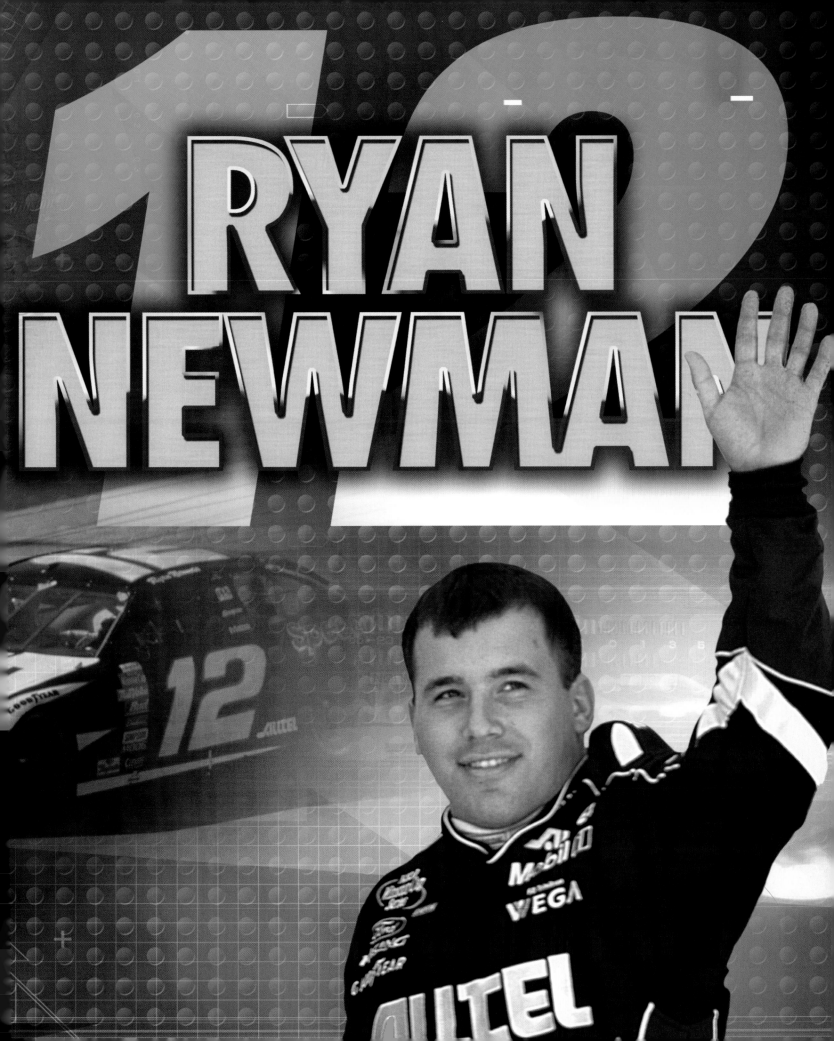

The Road to Stardom

Three years ago Ryan Newman was virtually unknown to many people who follow Winston Cup Series racing. Midway through his first season at NASCAR's top level, Newman has shocked everybody with his success while watching the bandwagon of fans grow larger by the day.

Make no mistake about Newman's talent: the 24-year-old Indiana native has more than proven to be the real deal behind the wheel of the No. 12 Alltel Ford. With a car owner like the legendary Roger Penske and a teammate like 1989 Winston Cup champion Rusty Wallace, Newman has entered his rookie season with all the top tools and equipment needed to get the job done.

"I'm just pushing the pedals; it's not all me," explained the modest Newman.

Even though Newman wasn't a household name a few years ago, his meteoric rise from the ARCA ranks through the Busch Series and finally into Winston Cup has been nearly flawless. After 18 of the 36 races that make up the 2002 Winston Cup tour, Newman sat an impressive 12th in the standings with two poles and a victory in The Winston all-star race at Lowe's Motor Speedway.

Though The Winston is a special event with no points on the line, Newman earned a lot of money and a ton of respect with his convincing win at the famed 1.5-mile Charlotte oval. As far as getting that first points victory, Newman

knows it's only a matter of time before he makes it to victory lane.

"The way we've been running, I don't think it's far away," Newman said. "I've felt that for a while. We have had mechanical failures and some driver errors, which I guess are all the things that are supposed to happen sometimes in a rookie season. We're just trying to do the best we can to minimize those and, hopefully, we can just have a good day one Sunday."

One of the only real problems Newman had in 2002 was competing with the performance of fellow rookie driver Jimmie Johnson. Despite putting up numbers that would easily be good enough to win the Winston Cup Rookie-of-the-Year award in almost any season, Newman was beaten by Johnson in 11 of 18 races. As a result, Johnson picked up two victories that allowed him to lead Newman in the race for the top-rookie honor by a 265-237 margin at the halfway point.

Newman is as smart off the track as he is behind the wheel. He recently graduated from Purdue University with a degree in vehicle-structure engineering while still racing on weekends.

"He's a very intelligent, soft-spoken, seat-of-the-pants kind of driver," said Don Miller, cofounder of Penske Racing South. "He's a hardworking kid who has applied himself and brings an engineering approach to racing."

Newman is among an elite few drivers to reach the Winston Cup level during the last 10 years without a tremendous amount of past success in NASCAR. Yet he has still been an

immediate threat for wins and a championship. Since four-time Winston Cup champion Jeff Gordon came into the series full time in 1993, more than a few team owners have seen that youth is the way to go, despite their lack of experience.

Dale Earnhardt Jr. topped Matt Kenseth for rookie honors in 1998, with both winning races. Tony Stewart followed the next year and had the most successful rookie season in Winston Cup history with three wins, backing that up with six victories in 2000. The floodgates were opened for young drivers like Newman, Johnson, Kevin Harvick, and Matt Kenseth.

Is the Winston Cup Series becoming a young man's sport? If so, many longtime insiders feel that's not necessarily a bad thing. A recent NASCAR study conducted by an outside marketing agency reported that the fan base grew by 19 percent from 2001 to 2002. The study also found that 32 percent of NASCAR fans are in the coveted 18-to-34 age range.

"The natural development of younger drivers has come along at a good time when the national economy is down," said Charlotte-based sports marketer Max Muhleman. "It gives marketers a renewed reason to stay focused on NASCAR."

Lowe's Motor Speedway President H. A. "Humpy" Wheeler agrees that the youth movement has had a positive impact on the sport.

"This youth movement will do several things," Wheeler said. "It will drop the retirement age. I don't think you will see drivers racing into their fifties. It is going to continue to develop a certain demographic. I'm delighted."

As are many new fans of the Winston Cup Series.

Winning Through the Ranks

While many of the veteran drivers Newman competes with on a weekly basis do have years of racing experience, his own resume is short but rock solid due in large part to the time he spent pursuing his college education.

Newman is the only full-time driver in Winston Cup racing with a four-year college degree. The desire to race has always been in Newman, who competed in Quarter Midgets at age four and eventually rose to the USAC ranks in 1995.

"My dad always wanted to race but never had the chance," Newman said. "When I was offered the opportunity, he gave me his full support."

Newman started on his path to Winston Cup racing in 1999 when he won the USAC Silver Bullet Series national championship with two victories. That same year he also won seven Midget races and one Sprint race. Newman has since been enshrined into the Quarter Midget Hall of Fame.

In 2000 Newman made his stock car debut at Michigan in an ARCA race and finished seventh; he then won in only his second career start at Pocono. Roger Penske's vision for Newman was tabbed as the "ABC Plan"— meaning a short stint in ARCA and one year in the Busch Series before being moved up to Winston Cup racing in 2002. One of Newman's biggest assets was having retired racing legend

Buddy Baker as his personal mentor and driving coach.

Following the ARCA win at Pocono, it only got better for Newman as he reeled off victories at Kentucky and Charlotte. In fact Newman still holds the track record at Charlotte with the fastest speed in a stock car at 186.780 mph in his ARCA entry.

"It was a pretty eventful race," Newman said following his October 2000 victory at Lowe's Motor Speedway. "The guys on my team did an awesome job. They are what make me look so good. My success is based around my crew, the Penske organization, and Buddy Baker. We had to fight hard at that Pocono race and we had to fight real hard to come through the field in the Kentucky race. It by |no means has been easy."

His fellow ARCA competitors begged to differ.

"It's like we're running for second," veteran driver Bob Strait joked of running races Newman entered that season.

It was becoming clear that Newman had superstar potential and was ready to proceed to the next level.

"His performance was way beyond our expectations," team co-owner Don Miller said.

In addition to a 15-race Busch Series schedule in 2001, Penske fielded Newman in a limited Winston Cup schedule so he could maintain rookie status in 2002.

Newman shocked more that a few people when he won the pole for the Coca-Cola 600 at Charlotte in only his third career Winston Cup start.

"I never imagined it," Newman said. "My crew chief, Matt Borland, has done an awesome job. Matt has given me a comfortable car so I can just push the pedal."

As far as the Charlotte race went, that story was a little different; he led the first 10 laps before getting into the fourth turn wall on Lap 11 en route to a 43rd-place finish. Jeff Gordon was closely pursuing, but Newman took responsibility.

"It was just inexperience and impatience, I guess," Newman said. "I got a little loose and got up into the fence. I thought I almost had it saved there for a little bit, but then I ran out of racing room. Jeff was close and he might have taken the air off my spoiler a little bit, but it was nothing more than racing. Jeff wouldn't have done that and I didn't feel anything."

There would be better days ahead in his Winston Cup efforts as Newman finished second at Kansas City and fifth in the spring race at Michigan. Newman was also quite impressive in his Busch Series showings, picking up a victory at Michigan and eight top-ten finishes to go along with six poles.

"We made quite a few notes and gained a lot of experience," Newman said. "Me as a driver, I've learned a lot, too."

When Newman came into Winston Cup he had one benefit on his side (unlike most other first-year drivers). When the Penske team released former driver Jeremy Mayfield earlier in 2001, Newman vacated that open seat on the No. 12 Ford so he could fall back on team-owner points earned with Mayfield and later with fill-in driver Mike Wallace.

That's a huge advantage, because if a driver slips in qualifying in the first four races of the season, he stands a chance of failing to make a race. Newman had that luxury in his favor, but he qualified so well that he didn't have to use the provisional option a single time.

It proved to be a sign of things to come.

A Rookie Winner

If you ask Ryan Newman what the biggest win of his racing career has been so far, look for him to point to his victory in 2002's The Winston all-star race at Lowe's Motor Speedway.

It's a race that rookies theoretically have very slim chances of even being a part of. To be a part of the show, a driver has to have either won a race or made it into The Winston by winning one of two qualifying races. Since NASCAR's annual dash-for-cash at Charlotte is held in May, there aren't exactly a lot of chances to make the race. Newman made his way into The Winston by leading all 16 laps of the last qualifier.

As the sun started to set over the Charlotte track and the lights began to glisten off the

cars, Newman began to assert himself as a force to be reckoned with. After the first 40-lap segment, which in 2002 saw drivers eliminated in a format twist, Newman had moved from his starting position at 27th to finish 20th and grabbed the final transfer position.

Becoming one of only 10 drivers to make it into the final 20-lap race with a $750,000 winner's check in victory lane, Newman quickly made his presence felt when he grabbed the lead from Tony Stewart on the fourth lap and pulled out to what seemed to be a sure victory.

Then Kurt Busch spun Robby Gordon to bring out a caution and bunch the field. With only five laps remaining, Newman jumped out to a tremendous lead once the green flag was back in the air; then NASCAR officials threw the yellow flag in order to get a little closer start between the leaders, since it is a nonpoint event.

Though Newman got another solid jump on the restart, it wasn't long before he glanced into his rearview mirror to see Dale Earnhardt Jr. closing in quickly. Earnhardt had fresher tires than Newman. With only two laps remaining and almost $1 million awaiting the leader in less than two minutes, Earnhardt Jr. tapped Newman and got him loose, but allowed Newman to regain control of his Ford. Newman then pulled away for the victory.

"This is awesome," said Newman, who earned nearly $800,000 that night. "It means a lot to me, but it will mean even more to me later. Dale Jr. could have hit me. I take my hat off to him. He could have done me wrong and went on to win the race. We just barely transferred in a couple of the races, but we kept working and when it came down to it I drove the wheels off it."

Earnhardt Jr. agreed that if he had been more aggressive there might have been a different winner, but said that wasn't the way he wanted to win.

"I could have done a lot of things different those last laps," Earnhardt Jr. said. "If I had to do it over, I am sure I could have won the race. I got into him and backed off because I didn't want to spin him and that was the race. I will probably run it over 100 times in my head. It's a lot of money, an awful lot of money. But it wasn't worth all the people that I'd have made mad by wrecking him to get it. Ryan had such a great engine that catching him was one thing and passing was another."

After the race was over, the young Earnhardt sprinted to Newman in victory lane to offer his congratulations.

"Good save," Earnhardt Jr. told him. "Enjoy it; this [stuff] doesn't happen all the time."

Ironically, Newman joined Earnhardt Jr. as the only two drivers to have won The Winston during their rookie season. Newman also joined Michael Waltrip as the only driver to score a victory in The Winston despite having to make the field through a preliminary race.

If Newman had a track that he'd call his favorite, it would have to be Charlotte. In addition to The Winston victory, he earned his first Winston Cup pole at the 1.5-mile oval for the 2001 Coca-Cola 600, won an ARCA race there, and also holds the track's stock-car qualifying record.

"This is a team sport, and if it wasn't for my crew, I wouldn't be in a position to do what we've done," Newman said.

Cool Under Fire

If someone had to describe Ryan Newman, the description would have to include the fact that his emotions almost always appear to be the same. It wouldn't matter if he had just won the biggest race of his career or if he had just finished dead last.

A man of few words, he always has that smile and a silent confidence. By looking into Newman's eyes you can see his passion to race, his focus on the task at hand, and nothing else. After he climbs out of his car each weekend, whether it's qualifying or race day, Newman wants to be able to talk to his team and crew chief Matt Borland. He always wants to know what they could have done to be better.

When you have the financial backing of someone like Roger Penske as a team owner,

losing is simply not an option—for the owner or his drivers. It appears that, in Newman, Penske has a potential superstar on his hands.

"I have a big learning curve ahead of me, but Roger Penske and Don Miller can provide me with all the resources I need," Newman said.

Penske is the majority owner of Penske South Racing, with Don Miller and Rusty Wallace sharing minority ownership. So far for Newman, it's been the chance to establish himself as a driver who will have to be dealt with in the future for wins and championships.

There are two more important people who have helped Newman reach the pinnacle of NASCAR. One of those is his teammate, former series champion Wallace, and the other is retired racing legend Buddy Baker.

Wallace has taken a vast interest in the engineering knowledge that his new teammate has, and many hours are spent debriefing between the two teams.

"Any driver would be crazy not to sit down and listen to what Rusty Wallace has to say," Newman said. "It's good to have had that as a resource. A lot of things we do on our team are very similar to what Rusty's team does. We will compare notes, setups, tire pressures, springs, shocks, track bars, and everything else to get the best package for both teams."

Newman holds a great deal of respect for Wallace both on and off the track.

"I'm racing another car, but I am a little more cautious with Rusty just out of respect," Newman said. "He owns a part of my team and part of his team, too, so there's no reason we need to beat and bang on each other. If one guy is faster than another, we can get out of the other's way, but overall we race each other just like we do everybody else."

At the halfway mark of the 2002 season Wallace was very much in contention for his second championship as he stood sixth and 171 points behind Winston Cup point leader Sterling Marlin. Newman, on the other hand, stood 12th after several strong runs that ended in disappointment.

"Rusty has been a great help," Newman said. "Just having Rusty Wallace help you around the track is great. I just thank him and thank all of my teammates for the opportunity—Don Miller, Roger Penske, and Rusty. Plus I've learned a lot as a driver."

Before and after reaching the Winston Cup ranks, Newman has done extensive test sessions with Baker, the winner of 19 races throughout his career.

"It's an honor to have someone of Buddy Baker's caliber, with his knowledge base from a driver's standpoint, because he can give me unlimited information," Newman said.

Another very important part of Newman's success has been Borland, who came on board with the Penske operation late in the 1999 season as an engineer. In April 2000 he was named Newman's crew chief and led him to three wins and two poles in only five ARCA starts. Newman also made his Winston Cup debut in November at Phoenix International Raceway.

Being a smart driver, Newman knows to give credit where it's due.

"We've definitely had a lot of good teamwork as far as the crew chief understanding the car I like to drive and what's fast," Newman said. "Matt Borland does an awesome job in understanding the physics of the race car and realizes what it takes to go fast. For me as a driver, it's a perfect situation."

Though things have gotten off to a much better start than anybody expected, Newman tries to keep it all in perspective.

"We're off to a great start as a team, and me as a driver," Newman said. "We've done some pretty special things. As a driver, I just need to keep focusing on doing the same thing and having the race car there at the end of the race so we can have good finishes."

Against All Odds

Ryan Newman wants to win a NASCAR Winston Cup Series championship and expects to be a regular contender along with Rusty Wallace. Newman knows he can pull it off, but he expects to do so sooner rather than later.

"We've always set the bar pretty high for ourselves," Newman said. "My team works really hard to give me the best possible car. By performing well we reinforce everyone's hard work. I think there are a lot of things that we are capable of doing. We as a team just need to take the rest of the season one race at a time.

"We want to do well and be consistent—that's what is the most important to us. I'm just fortunate to have the people and cars behind me that have allowed me to be so successful."

Wallace is convinced that Newman is going to be a fixture on the Winston Cup tour and that many victories and possible championships are in Newman's future.

"Unlike a lot of young guys coming into Winston Cup racing now, Ryan has done it the right way," Wallace explains. "He's smart and knows how to handle situations as well as or better than many of the veteran guys. Ryan shows tremendous respect for the sport. He's aggressive but not cocky. He also has a good attitude with a great personality. Ryan is already getting a real solid fan base behind him."

Newman has gone against great odds as a Winston Cup rookie. He has posted finishes that have left even the seasoned veterans a bit envious. Instead of worrying about making

races, Newman has now shifted his focus in gaining on Jimmie Johnson in the Rookie-of-the-Year battle and finishing amongst the Top 10 in Winston Cup standings by the 2002 season's end.

Despite having a tremendous first half of the season, Newman gave his team less-than-perfect grades in some areas.

"As far as performance goes, I give us an A- because our finishes haven't reflected our race performance," Newman said. "On reliability, I give us a C, and on overall performance a B. We have done well at every track, but have had errors of some sort, whether it's me punching holes in radiators or engine failures.

"We have a lot of learning to do and we knew that coming in. There have been frustrating situations where we think back and wonder if we shouldn't have done something differently. Overall, we're not doing bad for a rookie team with high expectations."

When asked what has been the key to his success, Newman again shifts to the modest mode.

"We learned a lot of things last year in both the Busch Series and Winston Cup Series. We have been able to carry it over pretty successfully into this season," Newman said. "We've done a lot things we did last year as far as qualifying packages goes, and sometimes you hit on that one thing and adapt it to every race track that was ever made. The success we are having this year is based on the results we created last year."

While it was a long shot for Newman to win the championship his rookie season, he most certainly will be a factor in 2003.

"Momentum is important to keep but easy to lose," Newman cautioned. "It's important to keep everything in perspective and make improvements. I'm fortunate to have the people and the cars behind me that allowed me to be successful. It's been gratifying to myself and my family to know that what I've worked for my whole career—my whole life really—is finally becoming a reality."

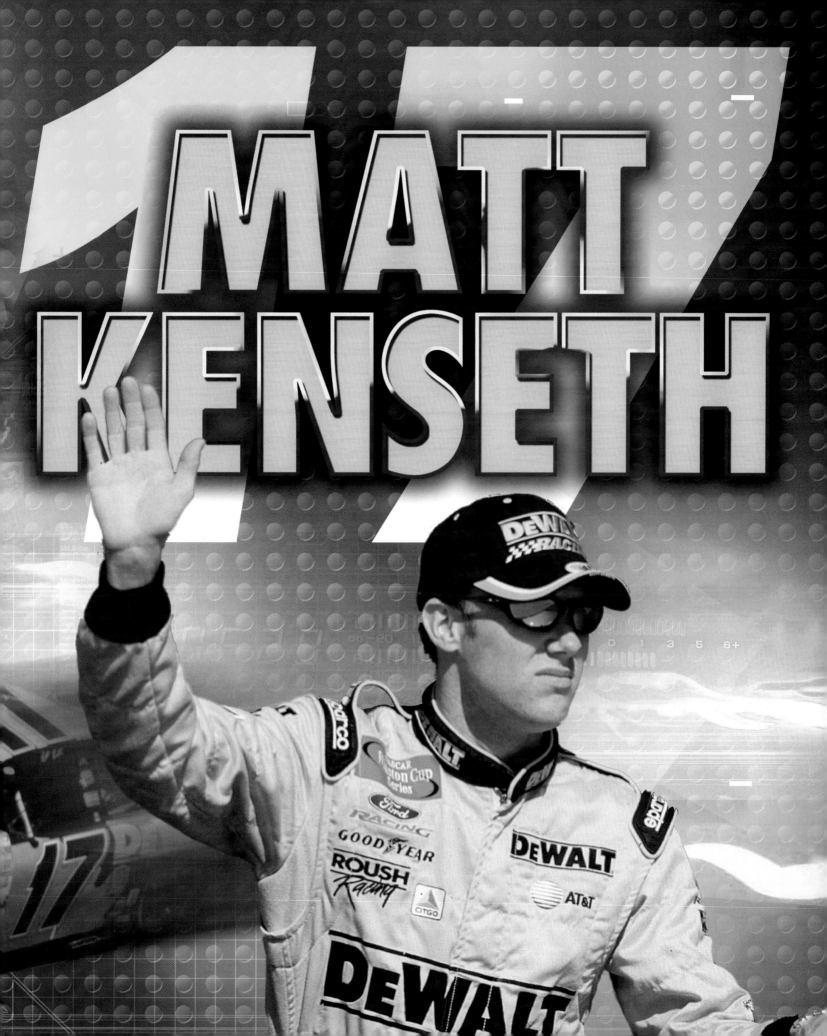

MATT KENSETH

The Man to Beat

Winston Cup driver Matt Kenseth hasn't been around the sport a long time, but through the first half of the 2002 season, he was the man to beat with a series-leading three wins.

Coming off a disappointing season in 2001 and not winning a race, Kenseth and the No. 17 DeWalt Tools team came out of the box on fire in 2002. They won in only the second race of the 2002 season at Rockingham, and you could literally hear a sigh of relief coming from the cockpit of Kenseth's car after starting the year with a win to snap a 59-race winless streak.

"This is only the second one of these things I've been able to win, and it's really difficult," said Kenseth, who admitted his confidence

took a beating in 2001. "I always wondered if I'd ever win again. I'll do the same thing after this race and wonder if there ever will be a next one because you never know. It felt like 160 races. It felt like forever. When we won Charlotte so early our rookie year that set the bar high. That's a pretty difficult race to win and then we ran really well the next few weeks.

"Then our performance just started dropping off and it continued through 2001. I was hoping that we would come back out of the box strong this year and keep improving our performance. I felt real good about that."

The 2001 season as a whole was not a good one for the Roush Racing camp. With their four-car Winston Cup operation, they only

produced two wins. Jeff Burton won both of those races, while teammates Kenseth, Mark Martin, and rookie Kurt Busch were winless.

According to team owner Jack Roush, his teams' problems in 2001 seemingly came from out of nowhere.

"We kept telling ourselves all last year when one bad thing would happen after another that we had better race teams than that," Roush said. "The terrible things that happened, whether it was a parts problem or some other issue that we hadn't planned for or anticipated, caused us trouble. That was not the norm and I knew we could do better than that. This business ebbs and flows.

"We certainly got less for our effort in 2001 than we had gotten in the past for the same effort. I just hope we'll continue to have the good fortune from now on. This is going to be a long year and to be able to have a good start in 2002 rather than the start we had last year, it's makes me sleep better at night."

For the most part, Roush's organization was showing a drastic improvement in 2002. Only four races after Kenseth won at Rockingham, it was rookie driver Kurt Busch picking up his first career victory in the spring race at Bristol. Mark Martin then pocketed an extra $1 million by fending off Kenseth down the stretch to win the Coca-Cola 600 at Lowe's Motor Speedway. Kenseth would go on to pick up his second and third win of the 2002 season at Texas and Michigan, respectively. In fact, with half of the 2002 season remaining, Martin was very much in contention for what would be a first Winston Cup championship for him and

Roush Racing after many years spent together trying to reach the pinnacle of this sport.

The only driver really struggling through the first half of 2002 that was somewhat of a surprise was Jeff Burton, the only driver outside the top-10 in points with no wins—and 18th in the standings.

While Roush was sleeping better than in 2001, so too was Kenseth.

"A lot of it is just circumstances and luck," Kenseth said of the improvement. "One thing I can tell you is our cars have handled much better than they did in 2001 when we were driving 20th-place cars most of the time. No matter what the circumstances are, if I'm in a 20th-place car, I'm not going to win races. The car has got to be fast and you've got to have everything going your way to win because it is so competitive.

"I'll never underestimate how competitive it is again. It's so easy to get a little bit off. I think five years ago you could be a little off and run fifth or sixth or seventh if you were a top team. Now if you get a little bit off you can easily run 20th or 25th on a good day. It's just really difficult and so competitive. You've got to have everything right, but so far this year everything has worked out for us."

Along for the Ride

A few short years ago at Talladega, while racing in the Busch Series, a young Matt Kenseth gained the attention of veteran Winston Cup driver Mark Martin, who took a keen interest in a driver he thought had the chance to become one of the future greats.

Kenseth came into the Busch Series after the 1997 season had already started, driving for a team owned by Robbie Reiser, his current Winston Cup crew chief. Though he came on board with the Reiser team in mid-April, Kenseth finished a respectable second in the 1997 battle for top Busch Series rookie honors.

In 1998 the duo of Kenseth and Reiser got the chance to move to Roush Racing for a full Busch Series season with some of the best equipment in NASCAR. Kenseth performed masterfully and made Martin look like a genius when it came to picking young talent.

At Kenseth's side the whole time, plotting strategy and calling the shots, has been Reiser.

"With our Busch team and all the things me and Matt have been through, we've been through a lot together and have a very good relationship," Reiser said. "Matt is a great driver. He's always done a great job and been a pleasure to work with. I enjoy working with him a lot because he's got the talent and he knows what he's doing. He's done a really good job not just as a driver but also as a real good friend of mine."

After all was said and done at the end of the 1998 season, Kenseth and Reiser had picked up three victories and finished second in the Busch Series championship race to Dale Earnhardt Jr. In 1999 Kenseth again finished second to Earnhardt Jr. in the final Busch Series standings with four victories.

According to Kenseth, the working relationship that he has shared with Reiser in the Busch Series played a major part in their success and eventual climb up the Winston Cup ladder.

"We've been working together since 1997, and Robbie has been my only crew chief ever for Winston Cup or the Busch Series, so we've obviously had a good relationship together," Kenseth said. "We started this thing together, and we've been together for a long time. We have a great relationship and work really well together. The biggest thing between Robbie and me is that we have a lot of trust in each other. When he tells me he does something, I trust his judgment, and Robbie trusts me

when I tell him something. Robbie knows what I need and what I want."

As Kenseth's two full Busch Series had clearly shown, he was ready to move up into Winston Cup and battle with the best of the best. Roush knew that if he didn't get him into Winston Cup pretty soon, other team owners would be knocking on Kenseth's door with offers to go with them. Kenseth had shown incredible talent and gained notice in his first Winston Cup start at Dover in 1998 when he substituted for Bill Elliott and drove to a sixth-place finish.

Roush decided that not only would Kenseth move into Winston Cup for the 2000 season, but so too would Reiser and basically the entire No. 17 Busch Series team as well. Roush didn't want to break up the communication the team had built in two years of working together, figuring that if something wasn't broke, there was little need to fix things for Kenseth.

Roush's decision to move Kenseth and Reiser into Winston Cup on a full-time basis in 2000 proved to be a smart plan, as Kenseth won in only his 18th start by scoring the victory in the Coca-Cola 600 at Lowe's Motor Speedway. In doing so he became the first rookie in history to win NASCAR's longest race.

"Matt and that team are just doing an awesome job," Roush said. "Robbie has done a great job of leading that bunch of guys to do what they've done so far."

With fireworks lighting up the sky above the Charlotte track following Kenseth's Coca-Cola 600 and while Kenseth was celebrating in victory lane, Martin was behind the scenes sporting a wide grin.

"That's awesome," Martin said. "It's just fantastic."

For Kenseth, Roush, and Martin, it was only a sign of bigger and better things to come in the future.

Exceeding Expectations

When Matt Kenseth burst onto the NASCAR Winston Cup Series circuit full time in 2000 for team owner Jack Roush, he brought with him great expectations from the fans and media alike.

The stir was not solely based on Kenseth because he was joined in the Rookie-of-the-Year-Award fight with fellow first-year driver Dale Earnhardt Jr., considered the favorite. The two young drivers first came to know each other while coming up through the Busch Series ranks, with both eventually becoming close friends away from the track.

At the track in the Busch Series, Earnhardt Jr. and Kenseth raced each other hard but clean and fair. Kenseth, far more reserved with often little to say if not asked, was considered the underdog against the splashy style of Earnhardt Jr. They say that opposites attract, and that has definitely been the case between the two drivers.

Kenseth and Earnhardt Jr. were the key reasons that fans who had just watched the Winston Cup races flipped on their televisions or radios to follow the Busch Series races. The two drivers competed in thrilling fashion throughout both the 1998 and 1999 seasons, with Earnhardt Jr. winning both titles while Kenseth would finish second and third, respectively.

Many expected to see that trend continue, but Kenseth was to have none of that and went on to beat Earnhardt Jr. and silence his critics

by winning the 2000 Rookie-of-the-Year Award in one of the closest races for that honor in Winston Cup history.

"Winning the rookie award is really cool, and it means a lot," Kenseth said.

According to Kenseth crew chief Robbie Reiser, he saw the fire in Kenseth's eyes as the duo completed a great first season in 2000, including the team and driver's first career victory in NASCAR's longest race—the Coca-Cola 600 at Lowe's Motor Speedway.

"Matt did a great job all year, but so did the rest of the guys on this team," Reiser said. "I'm pretty proud because this was a team effort and I'm excited to be a part of that. It's a pretty special deal for all these guys to win in one of the best rookie classes in a long time in Winston Cup."

Earnhardt Jr. had won earlier in the 2000 season at Texas to get his first Winston Cup victory, and backed that up a few weeks later by winning The Winston all-star race at Charlotte. But after Kenseth won the Coca-Cola 600 eight days after The Winston, the tide of the rookie chase started to shift the way of the Kenseth camp.

Earnhardt Jr. admitted that outside distractions and burnout became factors late in his team's struggles. While Kenseth had obviously brought attention and had high hopes, he didn't have the expectations that came with being the son of a seven-time Winston Cup champion. Earnhardt Jr. failed to finish 12 races and ended up 16th in points, with Kenseth not finishing five races to end up 14th in the final standings. Earnhardt's struggles allowed Kenseth to win the 2000 Winston Cup Rookie-of-the-Year Award by a mere 42 points over his close friend and on-track foe.

The Sophomore Jinx

After winning top Winston Cup rookie honors in 2000, Matt Kenseth could hardly wait to get his sophomore season under way. But the 2001 season ended up being one that he would just as soon forget. While he was getting valuable track time, Kenseth was rarely a threat to win and went the entire year without a victory.

It was a fact that wore on Kenseth, who posted only five top-ten finishes throughout the entire 2001 season before finishing 13th in the final standings.

"I felt like we had bottomed out," Kenseth said.

Roush agreed—his entire operation went through a disappointing 2001 campaign. When asked what specifically led to the problems,

Roush takes some of the blame personally while noting that a new and more-uniform tire introduced at the start of the 2001 Winston Cup season was also a factor.

"Goodyear gave us a great tire in 2001, but it threw us," Roush said. "Anybody that had any experience with the tires that were used before was lost for a while. We spent a long time trying to figure out if we had our tires screwed up—if we had forgotten what we needed to do with the shocks—or if the drivers weren't getting the right feel they needed out of their cars. It took a while to get all of that sorted out, so that cost us a lot of the 2001 season.

"We also broke some parts last year. We didn't run as well as we could on many occasions, some for hardware reasons that were my fault. When the season was over, we analyzed the things that had gone wrong to never do again. We also had a short list of things that had worked for us in 2001 that we wanted to continue to try and do in 2002. We didn't add more people or spend any more money. We just finally got a little more luck in having things go the way we needed them to go.

"Matt and the rest of my drivers have got more familiar with the tire to where they know what to expect from one track to the next so we could get settled down with our cars. In 2001 we had a myriad of car combinations. We were trying to pin the tail on the donkey to try to figure out what was going to stick. Heading into 2002, we had some pretty good cars we'd built over the winter."

Kenseth admits the comparisons between his cars from 2001 to 2002 have gone from the

bad end of the spectrum to some of the best rides on the track.

"Our cars have handled much, much better than they did last year," Kenseth said of the 2002 improvement. "Last year, we very seldom put ourselves in a position to win. You have to put yourself in that position to win. If you're running with the leaders and running up in the top five with competitive cars, you are going to win your share of races. That was my goal."

Crew chief Robbie Reiser agreed that they could never really get their chassis to match up to the new tire that was introduced in 2001.

"That pretty much explains it," Reiser said. "That's kind of why last season we struggled a little bit. We worked on it and we've got that part of it better and our cars were able to run lot better in 2002."

Even though the Kenseth team was a legitimate threat more races than not in 2002, Kenseth still saw room for improvement.

"I feel like we still have more work to do," Kenseth said. "We have good cars, but I don't think we can rest and say that as a team since we won three races that we're good enough and can leave everything alone. I still think we need to work hard and take every item that's going in our cars and make them the best we can make them. We've had great cars, but I still feel like there's room for improvement and we could be even stronger. That's a great feeling. When you can win races and know that you still have room to make your cars even better, that's a wonderful thing."

A Regular Contender

Just as Matt Kenseth made his contender status clear in the first half of the 2002 season with a series-leading three victories, Kenseth and the No. 17 team have also shown that they are going to be a player in many championship races in the future.

Though 2002 might not have been their year—sitting 10th in the standings and more than 250 points outside the lead—many expect big things in 2003 if Kenseth keeps up the pace and wins races on a continual basis. The team had set the bar high and planned to keep it that way.

Coming off his rough 2001 sophomore season, not many people gave Kenseth much chance of being able to mount a serious threat

for the 2002 title. However, after two of three early victories in 2002, Kenseth sat second in the Winston Cup championship race and a mere 27 in arrears to leader Sterling Marlin after eight races.

Then the bad luck that had plagued Kenseth and crew chief Robbie Reiser the year prior started to strike again. At Talladega, in the ninth race of 2002, Kenseth was caught up in a multicar crash and finished 30th while Marlin ended up 5th and padded his lead to 109 points. Rusty Wallace finished 8th to further close ground on Kenseth's hold on second place in the standings.

With just the slightest bit of luck, Kenseth could have picked up six victories through the

first half of the 2002 season. If the No. 17 team didn't rebound and win the title, it would in all likelihood look back to three races in particular that dropped it back to 10th in the standings at the season's midway point.

Kenseth led by 19 laps at Talladega before getting caught up in a 24-car melee. At Pocono, the No. 17 was again strong before being stymied with a 35th-place finish as a result of a broken transmission. After winning his first career Winston Cup pole at Dover, Kenseth was again in contention before blowing out a right front tire and finishing 40th.

Early in his career Kenseth has found out the hard way that some things in racing are simply out of his control.

"Sometimes it's hard to figure out why freak things happen," Kenseth said. "I feel like the things that we could control are some of the things we've been doing fairly good at. Our performance has been good more than it hasn't. We've just got to take it one race at a time and see how the points turn out."

While it was not totally out of the question that Kenseth could climb from 10th to take the lead in the final half of the 2002 Winston Cup championship race, it was highly unlikely though stranger things have happened. More realistically, Kenseth would likely be pleased with finishing somewhere around the top five.

The most important thing, according to Kenseth, was building a strong foundation in the second half of the 2002 season in order to come out as a serious threat for the championship in 2003. No matter what happens, Kenseth says he's proud of the way his team bounced back from the adversity of a winless 2001 season.

"We've had an outstanding season," Kenseth said. "It has been the best year we've had since we've been in the Winston Cup Series. This team has worked hard to get to this level and we intend to keep pushing week after week until we end up in the hunt for the championship."

Reiser believed one of the main keys to a championship bid in 2003 could be how his team performs in its second visit to a majority of the tracks in the final half of the 2002 season.

"We've definitely had some great performances this year," Reiser said. "We feel great to have won three races, but at the same time we would like to have won some of the ones we let get away. We've been really strong at most places in 2002 and look forward to returning to those tracks for a second time."

After watching the way the No. 17 team has come together at the Winston Cup level, Reiser feels as if they are going to be in championship contention for many years to come.

"We expect a lot," Reiser said. "I truly believe we have a championship race team and that Matt is a championship driver."

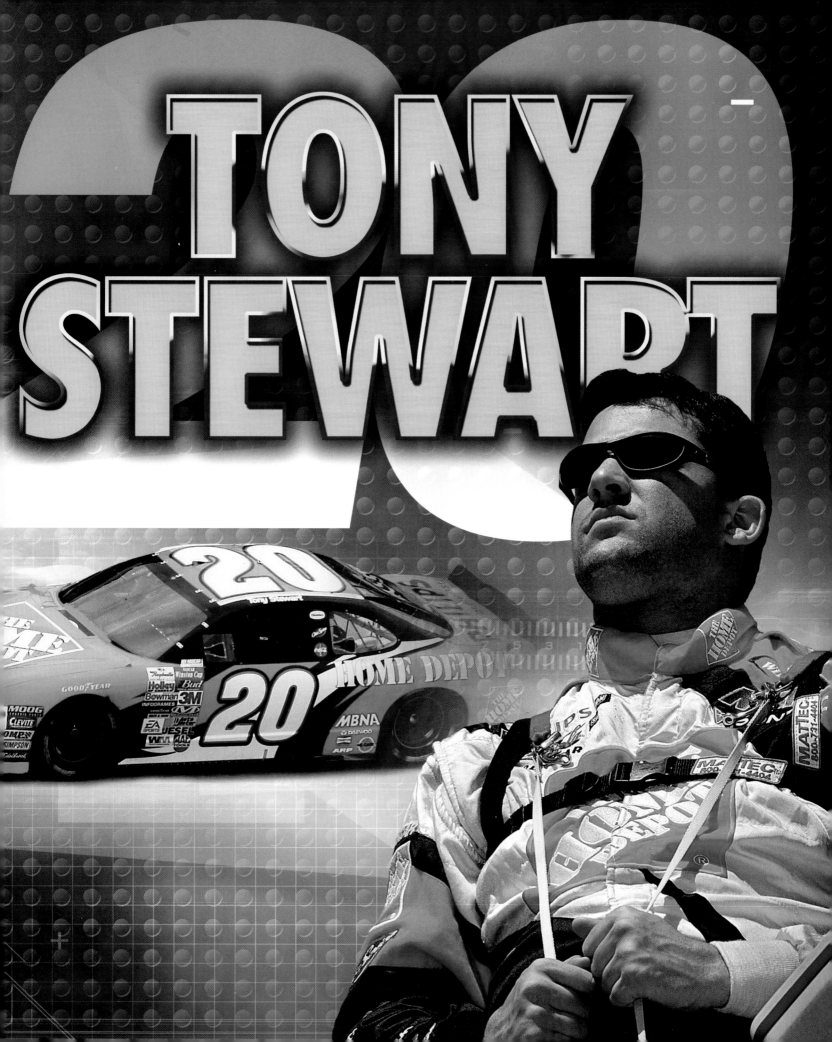

A Passionate Racer

When it comes to NASCAR Winston Cup Series competitor Tony Stewart, most race fans are on one side of the fence or the other about the driver of the No. 20 Home Depot Pontiac.

It's clear each racing weekend when Stewart's name is announced during driver introductions. He draws a response of some sort from everybody in the grandstands, be it good or bad. Some fans love his win-at-all-cost attitude while others could do without it. Whether you like him or not, Stewart has earned respect with 14 victories and counting in only four short seasons on the Winston Cup tour. Many felt that 2002 would be the year

that Stewart scored the first of several Winston Cup titles in what should be a bright career.

The late Dale Earnhardt once joked that if the fans weren't applauding or booing, the driver wasn't doing his job. Stewart is very much cut from that same mold, as he too seems to feed off his critics. Stewart has been called volatile, but so too have some of the greatest drivers in NASCAR history. If having a burning desire to win races and contend for championships is a crime, Stewart pleads guilty as charged.

"Being volatile doesn't make you a good driver," Stewart explains. "Winning races makes you a good driver. The distractions outside of the car are what make me volatile, so

I'm eliminating the distractions and probably won't be volatile this year."

Volatility is the very reason that Stewart has become so popular—racing fans are tired of drivers getting out of their cars after a bad day and saying things that are politically correct. If Stewart is asked what's on his mind, he will give an honest answer with little regard for saying the right thing.

However, saying what's on his mind has led to several problems off the track. One of Stewart's main problems has been dealing with some members of the motorsports media. Before the 2002 season started, Stewart vowed that would change.

"If it doesn't make the car go faster or doesn't promote Home Depot, I'm not doing it," Stewart said. "I'm not messing with it. I'm not messing with the outside distractions. I'll show you my contract. In my contract, it tells me what I have to do and what I don't have to do."

Stewart also has a simple request for the media: a cooling-off period before the interviews start—something that is commonplace for athletes in other professional sports.

"My challenge to the media is to give me 15 minutes of cool down time after a race," Stewart said. "If they give me that courtesy this year, I will give them what they need to get their job done. It's a two-way street. If the

media works with me, then I will work with them. If it's a distraction of what I'm trying to do, I'm going to cut it off. My job is to drive, and if any of it is a distraction to what I'm doing in the race car, it's going to be cut it off. There are a lot of people that have always known how to handle it. It's just that everybody [in the media] learning this deal and how to work with us in the garage. Once everybody figures that out, I think everybody will be happy with the results they get."

After several highly publicized tirades throughout his young career, Stewart has visibly taken a more mature approach in dealing with adversity. The competitive fire remains, but Stewart has learned that sometimes it's better to say nothing than to make remarks that could hurt the image of his sponsors and NASCAR.

Yet many of Stewart's fans like him not only for his driving skill but also for having the guts to speak his mind when he feels as if he's been wronged. Stewart believes the fans deserve candid answers. In all honesty, Stewart is simply saying things that all drivers feel the same way about but are too scared to speak up about.

"I believe the people who read what the media writes and prints deserve an honest answer to honest questions," Stewart said. "That's the way my stand has been up to this point, and it's always going to be that way. I'm not doing my job if I don't give honest answers."

Stewart is not above saying that there have been some things he's done while learning the

ropes at the Winston Cup level that he would like to take back.

"I've learned a big lesson in life," Stewart said. "I thought that once I got to this level, I'd have everything I wanted. I thought I'd be as happy as I could ever be. And at times, I have been happier than I ever thought I could be. But there have been times in the last year and a half when I have been more miserable than I have ever been.

"When I signed up with Joe Gibbs to come run Winston Cup, I thought I understood everything that was going to happen. Now I realize I knew so little about what was going to change in my life over a very short amount of time. I stay away from controversy now. I don't care if it's about the weather or whatever you want to complain about. I'm out of it. I'm just happy to not be a part of controversy anymore."

The Road to Stardom

To say that Tony Stewart's rise through the various ranks of motorsports has been phenomenal would be an understatement. It all started as a dream when Stewart was growing up in his hometown of Rushville, Indiana.

From a young age, Stewart was exposed to racing due in large part to living about an hour from the legendary Indianapolis Motor Speedway. To this day, Stewart still says his favorite driver of all time is A. J. Foyt, who drove to fame in the open-wheel ranks. Since his early exposure to Indy Car racing, many thought a career in that series would be a natural.

In 1983 Stewart became a champion in the International Karting Foundation's Grand National division. Four years later he earned the World Karting Association's national championship.

As Stewart ascended the racing ladder, many team owners began taking notice of his natural talent. It was in 1991 when Stewart tried his hand in the USAC (United States Auto Club) open-wheel ranks, winning Sprint Car Rookie-of-the-Year honors. He competed in several divisions that year, doing well in every type of car he drove. Stewart also picked up the Rookie-of-the-Year award by finishing an impressive fifth in the points race at Indianapolis Speedrome in the Midget Series. He also picked up his first USAC Midget victory on August 9, 1991, at the Speedrome.

After learning the ropes at the USAC level, Stewart reached stardom in 1994 when he won the national Midget championship thanks to five victories. At the time he was still trying his hand at the more powerful Sprint division, posting a runner-up finish in the famous USAC Silver Crown's Copper World Classic at Phoenix.

In 1995 Stewart became the first and only driver in USAC history to win the sport's "Triple Crown" of titles. He captured championships in the National Midget, Sprint, and Silver Crown divisions.

Stewart's lifelong dream of racing in the Indianapolis 500 was realized in 1996 when he moved up to the Indy Racing League. He made his debut at Indianapolis in convincing fashion by winning the pole at a speed of 235.837 mph around the legendary 2.5-mile track. Stewart led 43 laps of the race before falling short of the victory. He ended the season with an eighth-place finish in the final IRL point standings. In addition to his IRL efforts, Stewart had started to feel the lure of NASCAR stock cars and ran eight races in the Busch Series for Ranier/Walsh Racing.

According to Stewart, one of the defining moments of his career came when NASCAR team owner Joe Gibbs offered him the opportunity to drive his Busch Series car on a limited basis in 1997. In addition to his Busch Series efforts, Stewart also competed full-time in the IRL and won the 1997 series championship.

In 1998 Stewart shifted his focus to Gibbs' Busch Series program and ran 22 races while completing another full season in the IRL. With his NASCAR efforts, Stewart won two poles and posted five top-five finishes. In the

IRL, Stewart won two races and four poles while finishing third in the point standings.

Gibbs, a retired NFL head football coach, wanted a talented young driver to add to his racing stable as a teammate to Bobby Labonte for the 1999 season. His decision to move Stewart up into the NASCAR Winston Cup Series would make the former Super Bowl–winning coach look like a genius in another very different form of competition.

Not since Jeff Gordon broke into the Winston Cup scene in 1993 had a rookie excelled as Stewart did in his first season at NASCAR's premier level. While Gordon's rookie season was good, Stewart's was nothing

short of incredible as "The Rushville Rocket" won three races and finished fourth in the final standings. Stewart easily won the Winston Cup Rookie-of-the-Year award. Stewart's success also seemed to spill over to Labonte and the No. 18 team as he won a career-best five victories a year before winning the Winston Cup championship in 2000.

Showing his first season wasn't a fluke, Stewart won six races in 2000 and finished sixth in the final standings. The following year Stewart picked up three wins before finishing second in the points race behind four-time champion Jeff Gordon. An interesting parallel between Stewart and Gordon is that both drivers were raised in Indiana, and many people thought they would end up driving Indy-style cars. But as the 2001 season showed, the two were at the top of their game in NASCAR.

Another interesting note regarding Stewart and Gordon is that their success has opened doors for other young and talented drivers who had historically been told that it takes the skill of a veteran to get the job done. Even though Stewart and Gordon never experienced a great deal of success in the Busch Series, they have asserted themselves as proven commodities at the Winston Cup level.

Stewart might not have traveled the usual road to reach the pinnacle of Winston Cup racing, but his natural driving talent will keep him in winning contention for many years.

Rookie Phenomenon

The successful Winston Cup career of Tony Stewart really can't be traced to one race, due in large part to the success of his rookie season. Stewart set rookie records at tracks he had never seen before with three wins and an incredible fourth-place finish in the final 1999 point standings.

By winning Rookie-of-the-Year honors, Stewart joined an elite class of drivers that includes Richard Petty, David Pearson, Ricky Rudd, Dale Earnhardt, Rusty Wallace, Alan Kulwicki, Davey Allison, Jeff Gordon, and Jeff Burton. Stewart's overall first-year results were the best among this all-star cast of drivers.

As a reward for his efforts, Stewart earned almost $3.2 million. What many people don't

know is that he could care less about the money. For him, the chance to win is what wakes him up every morning.

Ignoring the "sophomore jinx," Stewart rebounded from a sluggish start during the 2000 season with six more victories. Stewart would end up sixth in the points, due to not finishing five races that year, while his Joe Gibbs Racing teammate, Bobby Labonte, won the Winston Cup title.

In 2001 Stewart finished a career-best second in the Winston Cup Series championship with only two victories. More important than putting up numbers in the win column, Stewart was racing with the consistency necessary to contend for a championship. He would post 15

top-five finishes throughout the course of the 2001 season, along with seven top-ten efforts. During the course of the year, Stewart would also win the Bud Shootout in Daytona and pick up his first victory in an International Race of Champions event at Michigan.

The numbers Stewart has put up on the board in three full seasons is nothing short of remarkable. At the start of 2002, Stewart went into the Daytona 500 with 12 victories, four poles, 40 top-five finishes, and 60 top tens.

SHINING CAREER MOMENTS

Tony Stewart remembers the greatest Winston Cup Series victory of his career not because of the track he was on or the stature of the race. He remembers it for the driver he beat in the closing laps to score the win.

Following his victory in 2001's night race at Bristol Motor Speedway, Stewart was asked if that win was the biggest of his career. Stewart thought about the question for a moment before his thoughts returned to the 2001 Budweiser Shootout at Daytona International Speedway, when he held off seven-time Winston Cup champion Dale Earnhardt, who was driving his legendary black No. 3 Chevrolet.

"Bristol is one of the most satisfying, but I don't think it's the biggest," Stewart explained. "I still think the biggest is beating Dale Earnhardt in the Shootout. It was more of a personal triumph for me than anything. It was cool the day that I won at Daytona. It was intimidating for me to see him back there, but at the same time I had to do my job. You know, he had more tricks in his book than anybody else. Then after we lost Dale, it made it even more special."

Only seven days after Stewart outdueled "The Intimidator," Earnhardt was killed in a last-lap crash in the Daytona 500.

Stewart says another of his most special wins came earlier in 2002 at Atlanta when he scored the victory in the NMBA 500 after another challenge from the Earnhardt racing family in the form of Dale Earnhardt Jr., who finished second. The Atlanta victory also marked Stewart's first Winston Cup win in a 500-mile race.

Of course the chance to go to victory lane and be called a winner at the Winston Cup level is something drivers always hold special. Stewart had picked up his first victory in NASCAR's premier division in fall 1999 by leading 333 laps before winning the Exide 400 at Richmond International Raceway.

As if to make sure everybody knew his Richmond victory wasn't a fluke, Stewart completed a wildly successful season with back-to-back victories at Phoenix and Homestead-Miami. Those wins allowed Stewart to become the first rookie in Winston Cup history to win three races. Stewart won a pair of poles in 1999 and 2000, but was shut out in 2001.

Stewart has won at virtually every type of track on the Winston Cup tour. While the Budweiser Shootout is a special nonpoints race, Stewart has proven he can win on the high banks

of Daytona. His ace in the hole seems to be short tracks, where he's earned three victories at Richmond along with wins at Martinsville and Bristol. Stewart also seems to excel on flat race tracks—as evidenced by wins at Homestead, Michigan, New Hampshire, and Phoenix.

TONY'S TEMPER

Losing is something that Tony Stewart really hates. Unfortunately for Stewart, much of the attention he has gained has been because of what some consider to be his bad temper.

One of the first times Stewart showed his emotional and passionate side was at Martinsville Speedway, when he and Kenny Irwin got into a bumping match with their cars. Stewart would end up getting the worst end of the stick as Irwin spun him entering the first turn at the Virginia short track. After his car came to a rest, Stewart climbed out and waited for Irwin's machine to come back around. Stewart wound up literally trying to jump into Irwin's car in retaliation.

Following Irwin's fatal 2000 crash at New Hampshire International Speedway, Stewart later commented that he deeply regretted his action at Martinsville.

Another of Stewart's high-profile blowups happened after a practice crash with Robby Gordon in preparation for the 2000 Daytona 500. In the moments that followed, a heated confrontation erupted between the two before they were separated in the Daytona garage area.

One of the most entertaining moments of Stewart's career came in the 2001 spring race at Bristol when Jeff Gordon bumped him out of the way for position on the final lap. An angry Stewart retaliated by spinning out Gordon's car as he was coming down pit road afterward. Stewart was fined $10,000 for his actions and placed on probation.

Later that same season, controversy again found Stewart when he ignored a black flag over a disputed on-track rule infraction in the July race at Daytona. Stewart finished the race without acknowledging the penalty, and afterward got into a heated confrontation with NASCAR official Gary Nelson and a member of the motorsports media. As a result Stewart was again slapped with a $10,000 fine and had his probation extended through the end of the 2001 season.

Stewart acknowledged some of his actions, though he still felt the penalty was wrong.

"While I disagree with the black flag penalty, I accept the fine and probation that NASCAR has issued to me as a result of my postrace conduct," Stewart said. "My behavior was inappropriate, and for that I apologize. For others I may have offended, I regret that also. I will continue to work with all those people who support me on handling these types of situations better in the future."

Many insiders thought Stewart got off too lightly, while others thought he might be briefly suspended. Stewart is the first to admit there are things that, over time, he will hopefully be more capable of controlling.

"There's been so many things that have happened," Stewart said. "I feel like I've done everything that I've needed to do, or in all reality, at least what I thought I should be doing. Some things I haven't done the right way, and those things I would do different. There's a whole list of things that I should have done different, but you learn as you go. When you get your NASCAR license, there isn't a manual that they give you on how to live your life as a Winston Cup driver. I'm just going a chapter at a time."

GIBBS TAKES A GAMBLE

Getting a chance at NASCAR's top level was the realization of a lifelong dream. Stewart credits two people who have played a major

role in his Winston Cup career. One of those is team owner Joe Gibbs, who gave him the opportunity to show his talent; the other is crew chief Greg Zipadelli.

If you're a Joe Gibbs employee, success is expected.

Before entering racing, Gibbs had already attained fame and glory by leading the NFL's Washington Redskins to three Super Bowls. There was always an interest in racing for Gibbs, thanks in large part to having grown up in North Carolina.

When he decided to enter NASCAR, Gibbs wanted a winner and took a chance on an unproven driver by the name of Dale Jarrett to start the 1992 season. The chance paid off as the pairing won the 1993 Daytona 500. While Jarrett would drive for Gibbs for three years, he left following the 1994 season to take a ride with Robert Yates. Again taking a chance on an unproven commodity with talent, Gibbs replaced Jarrett with Bobby Labonte in 1995 and won three races the first year. While Jarrett would eventually go on to win the title in 1999 with Yates, Gibbs was vindicated in 2000 when Labonte won the Winston Cup championship.

In 1999 Gibbs added Stewart as a teammate to Labonte. As his three-win rookie season proved, Gibbs had another winning team on his hands with Stewart and Zipadelli.

While other teams approached Stewart with offers of more money, he made his commitment to Gibbs crystal clear.

"You win three races in your rookie season, why would you go anywhere else?" he asked. "It's not all about money. I'd much rather take a smaller paycheck and win races then take a bigger paycheck and run in the back. We're pretty much married to each other now."

Racing Toward a Dream

Heading into the summer months of the 2002 season, Tony Stewart was off to a remarkably good start for a driver who was known to perform better as the year wore on. He picked up a pair of wins early in the year at Atlanta and Richmond after suffering a heartbreaking 43rd-place finish in the season-opening Daytona 500 due to a blown engine.

Instead of dwelling on the rough start, Stewart could only look ahead and hope.

"I think everybody is kind of realistic about the fact that with 36 races, any driver is going to have three or four bad days during the year," Stewart said. "You hope you don't have any, but being realistic, everybody expects to have three or four bad races. We just look at

Daytona as one of them. You hate to use that card up early, but you know that that is probably going to happen to some of these other people down the road."

Unfortunately, since his first year in Winston Cup racing, playing catch-up in the championship is something Stewart has become accustomed to.

"History has shown that we need to do better the first eight or nine races," Stewart said. "If we can do that and be fairly close to the front, we actually might have a shot at winning a championship. It seems like our weakness is the first eight or nine races."

Instead of struggling early in the 2002 season, Stewart witnessed a dramatic improve-

ment in his consistency. After leaving Daytona a devastating 43rd in the points, Stewart went on a rampage and moved from last to fifth in the standings. That fact had Stewart thinking that 2002 could be the year of his first Winston Cup championship.

"It really excites me knowing that we got off to a good start to the year and hopefully put ourselves in a position to where we might finally be there at the end of the season," Stewart said. "That right there makes me extremely excited about the possibility of what might lay ahead for us. We've just got to keep our nose to the ground and keep pushing. Hopefully, we'll get there before the end of the year.

"There are so many things that can happen. Do I think we're capable of winning the championship? Absolutely! We've won 12 races in three years and have had four poles, so yeah, we're capable, especially if you look at where we've finished in points the last three years— fourth, sixth, and second. Obviously, we are a contender, but it's just a hard situation to predict. I don't think anyone can honestly and accurately predict what's going to happen and who the contenders really are until it happens. There's a lot that can happen and a lot of variables can change as time goes on."

Having finished second in 2001's title fight to eventual champion Jeff Gordon, some see a natural rivalry growing between two of the best drivers in Winston Cup racing. Both drivers try

to downplay such a rivalry, citing a deep respect for the other's talents.

"It's not a rivalry," Stewart said. "I probably admire Jeff more than I admire anybody in this series by the way he handles everything. He's the kind of guy I look up to and model how I want to make my season work. With 43 guys, it's hard to create an individual rivalry between two guys. A lot of times the media tries to portray a rivalry more than there really is. You've got to remember that we race 38 weekends. We're with each other 38 weekends a year. It's just like a big, giant family.

"You've got so many people involved that eventually you're going to disagree with somebody along the line. But the next week, you kind of hit a reset button and start all over. That same person you had a problem with the week before may be the guy that helps you or you help him out the next week."

Gordon has admitted that despite his past differences with Stewart, he sees a driver as driven to succeed as he is.

"To me, what stirs up a rivalry is the fans," Gordon said. "Anybody who is competitive week in and week out and makes you battle them for the championship, that to me is your stiffest competition. I don't like the word rivalry. If Tony and me continue to run well like we have in the past, I'm sure we're going to have some more battles, but that doesn't mean we have to bump and bang and all that. We are two very competitive people who want to run good and finish good."

Through the years, Stewart's approach to life has become somewhat mellowed with more thoughts on how he wants to be remembered when he is no longer a part of the Winston Cup picture.

"I don't care if I die a millionaire or with 10 cents in my pocket," Stewart says. "I want to be a good husband some day, and a good father. I also want people to say I was a good person when I die."

Make no mistake about Tony Stewart: he is driven to succeed. Losing is not something he takes easily. As it stands now, Stewart longs to become the best of the best and win the Winston Cup championship.

"I don't care about the money," Stewart said. "All I care about is putting trophies on my shelf and winning championships. I'm very passionate in what I do. This is what I've dedicated my whole life to doing and I want to be good at it."